THE COLDWATER MARINE AQUARIUM

BIOGEOGRAPHY, ECOLOGY & HUSBANDRY

The Coldwater Marine Aquarium: Biogeography, Ecology & Husbandry
by Kenneth Wingerter

Copyright © 2016, Foreshores Publishing
Print ISBN-13: 9781533088710
Ebook ISBN-10: 1533088713
First printing: 2016

All rights reserved. Except for brief quotations for review or educational purposes, no part of this publication may be reproduced without the express written consent of the publisher and author. All inquiries should be addressed to kennethwingerter@yahoo.com.

Front cover photo by Chad King.
Title page photo by Arrested Decay Imagewerx.
Above photo by Oregon Department of Fish and Wildlife.
About the Author photo by Kenneth Wingerter.
Back cover photo by Ian Skipworth.

Contents

Preface *1*
Foreword *3*
I. Physical Geography *5*
1. Global Positioning *5*
2. Solar Energy *6*
3. Wind and Oceanic Surface Currents *8*
4. Waves and Tides *10*
5. Thermohaline Stratification and Deep Ocean Currents *13*
6. Upwelling *14*

II. Biological Geography *16*
1. The Marine Biome *16*
2. Coastal Habitats *19*
3. Major Regional Biotopes *22*

III. Marine Ecology *28*
1. Food Chains/Food Webs *28*
2. Primary Production *29*
3. Secondary Production *31*
4. Nutrient Allocation *33*
5. Distribution and Zonation *34*
6. Community Structure *37*

IV. Aquarium Systems *43*
1. Conceptualization and Planning *43*
2. Tanks and Cabinetry *44*
3. Sumps and Refugia *47*
4. Plumbing *48*
5. Pumps, Water Movement and Aeration *52*
6. Filtration *55*
7. Sterilization *62*
8. Temperature Control *64*
9. Lighting *67*
10. Electrical Systems *69*
11. Aquascaping *70*

V. Aquarium Hygiene/Water Quality *73*
1. Basic Water Parameters *73*
2. Water Changes and Cleaning *79*

VI. Aquarium Species *81*
1. Natural History *81*
2. The Microbes *84*
3. The Flora *87*
4. The Fauna *88*
5. Livestock Acquisition *99*
6. Acclimation, Quarantine and Conditioning *101*

Afterword *104*
Bibliography *106*
About the Author *109*

Preface

The marine Aquarium is, as yet, a plaything, a mere toy; but it is destined to become a far more important means of advancing science, and ministering to popular instruction, amusement, and wonder, than is yet dreamt of. It has yet to do for the ocean that which our menageries and vast gardens, devoted to the service of natural history, have done for the forests and mountains of the terrestrial portion of our planet. (H. Noel Humphreys, *Ocean Gardens: The History of the Marine Aquarium*, 1857.)

A quick glance at the bookshelf of any serious aquarist would lead one to conclude that there are more than enough works out there to satisfy the needs and interests of any tropical marine aquarium enthusiast. Be that as it may, copious volumes of neoteric material in the form of books, magazines, blogs and webcasts continue to be generated for this audience month after month of each year. Conspicuously absent, on the contrary, is a single, truly comprehensive treatment of coldwater marine aquarium keeping. In light of the mindboggling diversity and complexity of coldwater marine habitats for the aquarist to replicate, this creates a considerable void. Perhaps this obliviousness comes from an uneducated assumption that temperate aquarium livestock is somehow less desirable than that of the tropics; if we are to believe *Saltwater Aquariums for Dummies* (2002), these flora and fauna "come in fewer varieties and are less colorful than their southern friends." Still, bearing in mind the fact that the first marine aquaria were *coldwater* marine aquaria, the overall scarcity of literature devoted to their specialized care may seem puzzling.

In truth, part of this may be due to the relative newness of coldwater marine aquarium keeping as a distinct area of study. By the time mid-20th Century innovations such as undergravel filters had begun to make marine aquarium husbandry simple [*sic*] enough for the masses, advancements in air transport were allowing ornamental fish suppliers to flood the trade with exotic, tropical specimens from afar. Accordingly, the tropical marine aquarium hobby exploded (and still grows to this day) while its coldwater counterpart stagnated (until quite recently). In the mid-1980's, just as coral reef aquaria were really becoming a thing, Dick Mills (1987) addressed this paradox: "It is safe to assume that the greatest numbers of tropical fishes are kept by hobbyists in temperate regions far removed from the fishes' wild origins. If this is so, then shouldn't we try to redress the imbalance a little by turning our attention to the varied aquatic life around our own shores?" David Wrobel (1991) puts it in decidedly plainer terms: "The irony is that it is far easier for most people to obtain animals that originated thousands of miles away than it is to get those residing at our doorstep." Pioneering temperate aquarist Steve Weast (2004) once described this persistent dearth in the trade by pointing out that "there are no coldwater suppliers because no one has a coldwater tank and there are no coldwater tanks because there are no suppliers of livestock." It could be that a similar causative dilemma—the shortfall of updated, in-depth information on the subject in a readily accessible print format—has similarly hampered popular interest.

Just as specialized suppliers of coldwater marine livestock and products have at last risen to nurture the burgeoning demand, it is sincerely hoped that this work fills the gaping void in aquarium literature. It is specifically to the need for instruction of keepers of coldwater marine life, whether hobbyist, dealer, public aquarist, aquaculturist, laboratory animal technician or fisheries biologist, that this work is directed. While diligent internet searches, trips to the local library and well-placed phone calls can all be very good sources of information (such sources have certainly informed this work), they are seldom very practical. So, more than anything, we have sought to deliver nothing less than a truly comprehensive technical manual that can be *used*. A wealth of pertinent field data is given to assist in the recreation of distinct biotopes. A generous assemblage of full-color images provides many vivid examples of topics discussed in the text.

Perhaps most importantly, a considerable effort has been made to combine descriptive language and hard numbers in a way that most accurately depicts the complexities of coldwater seascapes. The emphasis on biogeography in this book is strong, and not inadvertently so. Arguably, any serious marine aquarist should be at least a little conversant with certain fundamental oceanographic and ecological concepts. In that respect, it is hoped that this work serves well in rounding out the bookshelf of frankly any kind of aquarist. But it is especially incumbent upon temperate and deep-water marine aquarists (who have a special penchant for biotope aquaria) to have some biogeographic knowledge of the marinelife in their keep. And, knowledge expands the imagination. To that end, I really hope that at least some readers, upon recalling the discussion on wind-driven surface currents, might actually imagine an upwelling event as they pour bottled nutrient supplements into their aquarium waters (the making of stormy ocean sounds is optional).

It is fair to say that coldwater marine aquarium keeping has advanced considerably over the last century. Philip Henry Gosse.

A truly complete printed reference on the subject would take a lifetime to write, if not to read. What I have tried to achieve with this book is to provide a practical overview of the major aspects of modern coldwater marine aquaria. I do not at all believe that I have presented the complete and final word on the subject; rather, I fully anticipate that much of the information contained in this text will be refined and augmented along with ongoing developments in the art. Despite being a fairly arcane pastime until recent days, coldwater aquarium keeping has grown to accommodate a multitude of highly involved and connected adherents; countless innovations in temperate and deep-water marine aquarium husbandry are all but destined to come. New and improved technologies will hit the market. Advanced techniques and methodologies will be conceived, tested and proven. Aquarium fish collectors will continue to brave rougher and deeper seas in pursuit of novel species. And, conceivably many new, intriguing coldwater marine habitats are yet to be discovered and described. So, while I do hope that my own modest objective has been suitably met, I also look forward to the many fine guides on the subject that are sure to follow in due time. How gratifying it will be if this work has inspired any of them...

Foreword

...for whatever we lose (like a you or a me) it's always ourselves we find in the sea. (e.e. cummings, maggie and milly and molly and may, 1956).

Is finding ourselves the reason why we go through the considerable effort of designing, building and maintaining the closed recirculating seas that we enjoy in our homes and businesses? Perhaps, but in order to find our selves we must first lose ourselves, which is alternately stressful and pleasurable. No matter how close an eye we keep on such things, the deadlines and dissonance in our daily lives often create stressors that cause us to compartmentalize and create distance from some of the essential parts of our selves.

However, getting lost becomes very pleasurable indeed when we park ourselves in front of our display tanks and drink in the beauty that aquatic plants and animals provide. Our blood pressure and heart rates drop, mundane concerns drift away and we get to immerse ourselves in that world for a while. I suspect that the readers of this book know this indulgence very well. They crave it, along with the satisfaction of accomplishing something that is challenging and technically difficult. While temperate marine life support systems are somewhat more challenging and difficult to construct and maintain than tropical systems, experienced aquarists who are ready to take on this challenge have never had more advantages to be successful.

Marine aquarists have been successfully keeping *Actinia* spp. anemones for well over a century. Michiel Vos.

It may come as some relief to know that professional aquarists also share many of the concerns that readers may have about closed temperate marine systems before they build and maintain these systems for the first time. In this book, the author makes this process intuitive and accessible, with practical information that builds on what aquarists already know. This information helps them avoid many of the setbacks that discourage and prevent people from taking their passion for aquatic animals in this new direction. It also provides insight into ways to proactively prevent these setbacks from happening.

If you've never worked with or maintained a chiller before, I can assure you that beyond the initial cost of buying a good one (and there is no point in trying to cut costs on this particular life support component) a little proactive maintenance, a good temperature controller, proper location of the temp sensor and a few other considerations are all you need to keep this device efficiently removing heat from your system for years.

Leery of the length of time it takes to properly cycle a temperate system? Unless readers have ready access to seeded biomedia, it will take extra time to establish their biological filtration but that extra time can be spent monitoring and addressing condensation, tweaking turnover and flow rates and monitoring water quality parameters. Once the system is cycled, the same considerations that help readers maintain good water quality in their tropical systems still apply.

Speaking of water quality, if readers are not in the habit of monitoring and proactively managing their parameters in a timely manner, setting up a temperate system is an excellent time to address this. While their eyes, experience and acumen will tell them whether or not an animal is getting the right kinds of nutrition in the right amounts, their water quality parameters will allow them interpret the overall health of their system and how effectively their filtration is removing excess nutrients. It will also inform their decisions on how often and aggressively to perform water changes.

Once the system is established, the usual petty frustrations and great joys of keeping aquatic animals are there for readers to see, feel and experience. However, I find that these joys are enhanced by the concomitant skill and patience required to get there. I've been caring for temperate systems and animals for many years and in my professional opinion, the same qualities that make aquarists successful in caring for tropical marine and freshwater systems will also serve them well when they take on this new challenge.

Indeed, the same eye for detail and assiduous work ethic that helped readers to get finicky freshwater fishes to spawn or allowed them to propagate and successfully frag out prized coral species will be instrumental in helping them succeed in this new endeavor. Suffice it to say that if you have been thinking about taking on the challenge of a temperate marine system, you will find this book an excellent resource, as well as an excellent read.

The work of Steve Weast has earned considerable praise from temperate and tropical aquarists alike. Steve Weast.

When e.e. cummings wrote the allegorical poem *maggy and milly and molly and may* in 1956, we were on the cusp of a breakthrough in our understanding of the world's oceans and the animals living in, on and around them. Jacques Cousteau was performing experiments and developing cutting-edge underwater filmmaking techniques on RV *Calypso*. In a few years, he would bring the wonders and breathtaking beauty of oceans and aquatic animals to our living rooms, broadening our perspectives and firing our imaginations.

If you are reading this book, you are likely on the cusp of a personal breakthrough of your own, ready to broaden your perspective and skills and bring the beauty of temperate animals into your living room. And you should, not only because temperate animals are pretty and interesting and the process is moderately difficult, but also because there is a unique and particularly satisfying kind of joy in losing one's self in a challenging endeavor. There might be an allegory or two in there somewhere, too. I think mr. cummings may have been on to something. I'm certain that Mr. Wingerter is.

Sid Stetson (Hatfield Marine Science Center), August 1, 2016.

I. Physical Geography
1. Global Positioning

A coordinate system of latitude and longitude is used to designate a location on the surface of the Earth, setting the orientation of North-South and East-West directions. There are 360 degrees of longitude (180° East and 180° West) and 180 degrees of latitude (90° North and 90° South). The planet's surface is intersected by the planetary axis at 90° latitude N and S, designating a North and South Pole. The equator, the longest longitudinal line, is equidistant to the poles. All longitudinal lines are parallel to the equator. The region between the equator and 30° is known as the low latitudes, while the region between 30° and 60° is known as the mid-latitudes and the region between 60° and the poles is known as the high latitudes.

A line that runs along the Earth's surface from pole to pole is referred to as a meridian. Because they converge at the poles, meridians are not parallel. The prime meridian, a line that intersects Greenwich, England, is by convention used as the zero of longitude. A nautical mile, a unit of measurement that accounts for the curvature of the planet, is set by international agreement as being exactly 1,852 meters (about 6,076 feet) or roughly 1/60 of the distance of 1° along a meridian.

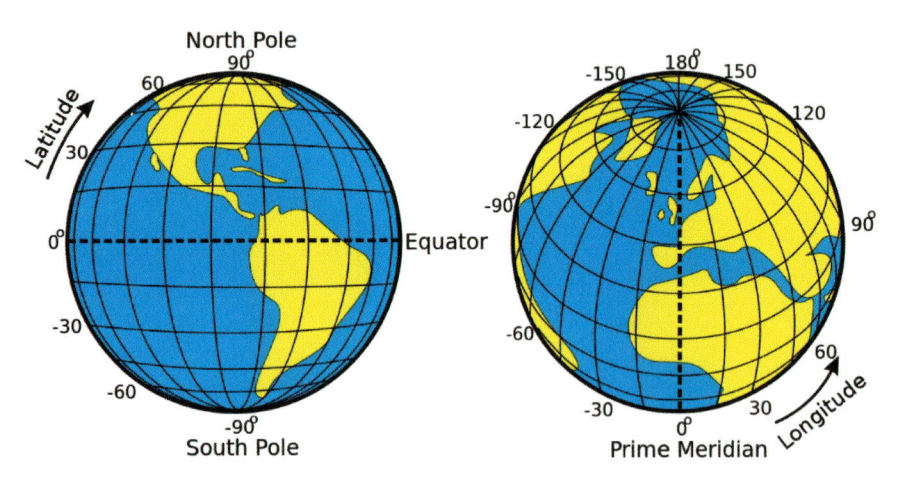

A geographic coordinate system allows any location on the Earth to be specified by a set of numbers. N, S, E or W are used to designate compass direction. Djexplo.

Looking down from the North Pole, the planet is rotating in a counter-clockwise manner; from the South Pole it rotates clockwise. The period of the Earth's rotation relative to the Sun (from true noon to true noon), referred to as a true solar day (or apparent solar day), averages something pretty close to 24 hours. Due to the eccentricity of the planet's orbit, this can be 29 seconds more or 21 seconds less than 24 hours of clock time. Whether at the equator or at one of the poles, the duration of one day (i.e. one full revolution of the planet) is about 24 hours. However, because the circumference of the planet is greater at the equator than nearer the poles, points along the equator move at a much greater speed than at higher latitudes.

An object on the Earth's surface moves in a circle as the planet rotates. As the object travels in a circular motion it experiences centrifugal forces that push outward as well as centripetal forces that push inward. The balance between these two forces is undone if the body changes speed. Increasing the speed draws the body away from the center of rotation; reducing the speed draws it toward the center. On the surface of the Earth, north-south speeds depend only upon the amount of force of the motion, while east-west speeds depend additionally upon the speed at which the body was spinning around the planetary axis when it was set into motion. This results in the deflection of north-south movement. In the Northern Hemisphere, horizontal movement is deflected to the right; in the Southern Hemisphere it is deflected to the left. The magnitude of deflection changes with increasing speed. The tendency to veer, therefore, is strongest toward the poles. Known as the Coriolis effect, this pattern of deflection is the cause of the curvature of major weather fronts in higher latitudes, exerting a powerful influence on wind and water currents across the globe.

2. Solar Energy

The Sun is 150,000,000 kilometers from the Earth—a relatively close proximity. The Sun emits 400 million billion billion joules of energy every second. Yet, for a number of reasons, our planet is not incinerated. Only a billionth of the energy released from the Sun reaches the Earth. Only about 50% of the sunlight that reaches the atmosphere strikes the planet's surface. The infinitesimal remainder of solar energy that is not reflected at the surface is absorbed and finally converted into heat.

The Earth completes its orbit around the Sun each 365.24219 days. This period is referred to as a tropical year (certain adjustments are made to calibrate the calendar for a 365-day year). The planet's axis is not perfectly perpendicular to the plane of its planetary orbit; rather, it has an axial tilt of about 23.4°. Due to the tilt, the position on the planet at which the Sun is directly overhead changes over the course of an orbit. The region between 23.5° N and 23.5° S is known as the tropics. These two latitudes are referred to as the Tropic of Cancer (to the north) and the Tropic of Capricorn (to the south). The Sun is most often directly overhead in the tropics, where the Earth's surface is almost perpendicular to the path of sunlight. In the Northern Hemisphere, a summer solstice (the longest day of the year) takes place June 20, 21 or 22; winter solstice (the shortest day of the year) takes place December 21 or 22. Solstices occur also in the Southern Hemisphere during these periods, albeit with winters and summers switched. The Sun is directly overhead at the tropic of Cancer during noontime summer solstice in the Northern Hemisphere and it is directly over the tropic of Capricorn during noontime summer solstice in the Southern Hemisphere. The sun lies directly over the equator only during the spring (or vernal) and fall (or autumnal) equinoxes (March 22 and September 22). The Vernal Equinox in the north coincides with the Autumnal Equinox in the south and vice versa. Seasons are caused by climatic patterns that arise from annual fluctuations of light intensity and day length. The terms tropical, temperate and polar are used to describe the prevailing temperature regimes of the lower, middle and higher latitudes respectively.

Though the average global surface temperature (over combined land and ocean surfaces) is 15°C (59°F), regional average temperatures vary significantly. Regional surface temperature differentials are caused primarily by the variable amounts of solar radiation absorbed at different latitudes. The angle of sunlight interception increases with increasing latitude. Sunlight strikes the earth more obliquely toward the poles, which extends the path of incoming radiation through the atmosphere and spreads it out over a greater surface area. Surface features that face away from the winter sun (to the south in the Southern Hemisphere and to the north in the Northern Hemisphere) will experience the least exposure. Even more sunlight is lost through reflection at higher latitudes (particularly nearest the poles) where there is extensive ice cover. Consequently, total annual insolation at the poles is around 40% less than at the equator. The equator and poles are subjected to prolonged extremes of high and low temperatures respectively. The highest average surface temperatures can be found along the equator while they are lowest at the poles. Surface water temperatures range from -1.9°C (28.5°F) in the polar regions to over 30°C (86°F) in the tropics; they hover near 0°C (32°F) in the former region and are usually a bit above 25°C (77°F) in the latter. The per-year influx and efflux of heat are equal only at 30° to 40° N and S.

The term temperate is used to describe a climate or region that is moderate in respect to temperature. Hence, much of the land and sea that falls within the midlatitudes is referred to as the Temperate Zone. The region between the Tropic of Cancer and the Arctic Circle (23.5° to ~66° N) is referred to as the North Temperate Zone; the region between the Tropic of Capricorn and the Antarctic Circle (23.5° to ~66° S) denotes the South Temperate Zone. The warmer or cooler margins of the Temperate Zone may be referred to respectively as subtropical and subpolar or collectively as subtemperate. Note that while the *average* temperatures of temperate regions are rather mild, temperate climates are characterized as having the most extreme *swings* of temperature.

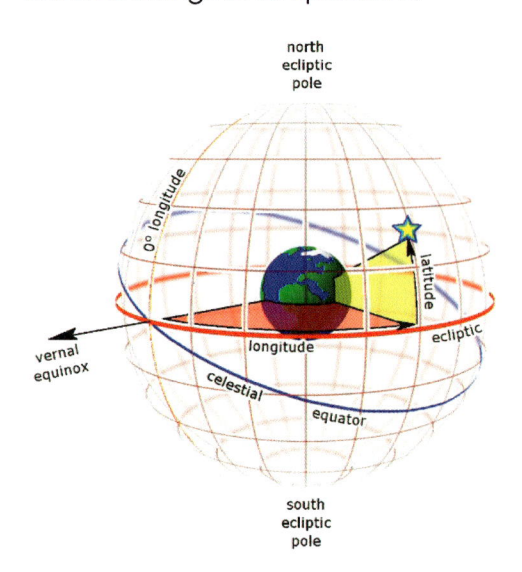

The celestial equator (a projection of the terrestrial equator into space) is inclined by 23.4° to the ecliptic plane. Tfr000.

There is an important difference between temperature and heat. The former is a measurement of the speed of movement of molecules (temperatures increase with faster movement), whereas the latter is a measurement that takes into account not only molecular speed but also the number of molecules. That is, temperature is a measurement of *average* thermal energy whereas heat is a measure of *total* thermal energy. Thus, while a 20-gallon and a 200-gallon volume of 13°C (55°F) water may be of the same temperature, the larger volume will contain far more heat. Due to the strong hydrogen bonds that hold it together, water has a high latent heat capacity. Just as evaporation absorbs heat energy, condensation releases it. The amount of heat required to raise the temperature of one gram of liquid water by 1 degree C (1.8 degree F), known as its specific heat, is very high at 4.186 joules. This is about four times that of air and is higher than all other common substances. In other words, water can store enormous quantities of heat.

Despite the absorption of intense noontime solar radiation, the surface water temperatures of open oceans usually do not change by more than 0.3 degrees C (0.5 degrees F) throughout the day. Even shallow coastal waters rarely change more than 2-3 degrees C (3-5 degrees F) in a day. The *annual* temperature range of oceanic waters at the equator is just 2 degrees C (3 degrees F). This increases somewhat with latitude to a range of around 8.5 degrees C (15 degrees F) around 50° N and S, but then decreases again toward the poles. In point of fact, seawater temperatures change much most dramatically with depth (i.e. vertically) than at different latitudes (i.e. horizontally). Based upon major global patterns of heat flux, the poles should be cooling and the tropics should be heating at a rate of about 10% per year. Yet, the poles do not continue to grow colder and the tropics do not burn up; average temperatures are, from region to region, fairly consistent from year to year. This is because the excess of heat absorbed between 30° and 40° N and S is equivalent to the loss of heat at latitudes nearer the poles. Thermal equilibrium is achieved through the large-scale transport of heat energy. Heat moves from the equatorial region toward the poles by way of a complex system of air and water currents.

3. Wind and Oceanic Surface Currents

Winds are responsible for about 50% of all heat flux on the planet. Wind gusts result from differences of air pressure, which result from differences of temperature. On a larger scale, variable solar heating at different latitudes drives the wholesale movement of air over the earth's surface. Due to its high heat latency, water absorbs and releases heat much more slowly than does air or land. Air pressure changes with altitude (at sea level, air pressure is 1.0×10^5 newtons/meter^2). When heated, air expands, which reduces its density. This causes it to float above the cooler, denser air around it (at room temperature, fully humid air is about 1% less dense than dry air). Sunlight warms the air over land masses faster than that over the ocean. The rising land air generates a low-pressure area into which cool ocean air flows. The resulting "sea breeze" peaks in the afternoon, when the difference between oceanic and terrestrial air temperatures is greatest; the reverse occurs in the evening hours while the land is cooling more quickly than the ocean, resulting in a "land breeze."

The equatorial low is an area between 5° N and 5° S that is characterized by very low atmospheric pressures. Intense surface heating in the tropics results in a belt of warm, humid air rising along the equator. Being less dense, warm air expands and rises while cooler air sinks; that is, cool air from high-pressure areas moves into low-pressure areas to displace the warm, rising air mass. This rising air expands as atmospheric pressure decreases. As it expands, it cools. As it cools, the water vapor condenses, forming clouds and rain. Heat stored in the water vapor is released during condensation, effectively being transported from one area to another. As it moves up into higher latitudes, it is deflected eastward by Coriolis forces. This generates jet streams in the vicinity of 30° N and S, by which point it has cooled enough to form a downdraft and begin sinking back into the lower atmosphere. This downdrafted air is very dry, often resulting in desert climates. Here, air may either continue on toward the poles or swing back toward the equator. This area of very high pressure from 25° to 35° N and S is referred to as the subtropical high. Winds blowing toward the equator from 30° N and S are deflected sharply. Owing to this, air returning to the lower latitudes, known as the northerlies (or trade winds) is carried in a southwest (in the Northern Hemisphere) or northwest (in the Southern Hemisphere) direction. Named for the direction they blow from, they are known respectively as the Northeast and Southeast trade winds. The flow of these winds is slowed by friction as well as reduced pressure at the lower latitudes, dropping in speed from 5-7 to 3-5 meters per second as they reenter the equatorial low. The region where the trade winds meet in the tropics and are forced to rise is known as the Intertropical Convergence Zone (ITCZ). Because there is a slightly greater heating of air in the Northern Hemisphere (there is more landmass, and terrestrial surfaces heat more easily than ocean waters), the ITCZ is actually situated around 5° to 10° N, rather than directly over the equator.

Wind driven waves are responsible for the intense mixing that homogenizes surface temperatures. Earth Network Editor.

Atmospheric circulation from 30° to 60° N and S behaves similarly. The air that moves to higher latitudes from 30° N and S is also deflected by Coriolis forces, creating the westerlies (which actually blow from the west). Humid air again rises to the tropopause at 60° N and S, where it is once more spreads northward and southward. A second jet stream blows to the east. This air again sinks as it approaches the poles, generating the polar easterlies. These massive, circular movements of air over the planet are referred to as convection cells; those that lie between the equator and 30° N and S are called Hadley cells, those between 30° and 60° N and S are called Ferrel cells and those between 60° and 90° N and S are called polar cells. The resulting pattern of precipitation is responsible for the concentration of desert at 30° and tropical rainforest at 60° N and S. Heavier precipitation reduces surface water salinity around the equator and 60° N and S. High-altitude air flows in Hadley cells as well as low-altitude winds from 30° to 60° N and S move heat away from the equator and toward the poles, while the trade winds and polar easterlies return chilled air to the tropics.

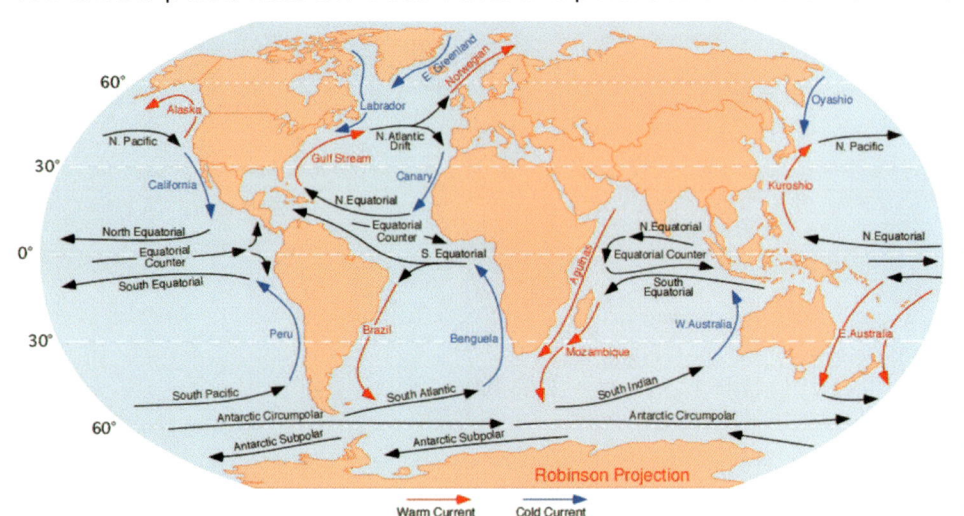

Sometimes, especially strong winds may circle around a low-pressure region, forming a cyclone. In the eastern North Pacific and Atlantic basin these powerful storms are referred to as hurricanes. During a hurricane, enormous volumes of air are rapidly sucked into the center of the low-pressure area, eventually assuming a recognizable spiral shape due to Coriolis forces. The weakest hurricane category (Category 1) exhibit wind speeds of 119-153 kilometers (74-95 miles) per hour and storm surges of 1-1.5 meters (4-5 feet) while the strongest (Category 5) have wind speeds of over 249 kilometers (155 miles) per hour and storm surges exceeding 5.5 meters (18 feet). Larger storm surges can lead to extensive flooding along coasts.

A complex system of currents crisscrosses the Ocean surface. Dr. Michael Pidwirny.

Though not always apparent from above the surface, ocean waters move across the globe in swift currents. This activity serves to move excess tropical heat into higher latitudes (e.g. the North Atlantic Drift which warms Northwestern Europe and the North Pacific Current which warms the Pacific Northwest Coast of the U.S.). The primary force that generates these oceanic surface currents is the planetary wind system. The trade winds, westerlies and polar easterlies are the main drivers of oceanic currents. The low-latitude trade winds drive the westward-flowing North and South Equatorial Currents. The mid-latitude westerlies drive the eastward-flowing North Pacific and North Atlantic Drifts in the Northern Hemisphere and the West Wind Drift in the Southern Hemisphere. The polar easterlies drive Oyashio Current in the Northern Hemisphere and the East Wind Drift in the Southern Hemisphere. In all, wind-driven surface currents account for some 10% of the ocean's water volume.

Rather than being directed by wind alone, global surface water movement is additionally shaped by Coriolis forces and east-west pressure gradients. The planet's rotation causes surface currents to flow at a 45° angle to the winds. North-south currents are generated as gravity and physical barriers (e.g. the continents) divert prevailing east-west currents. The resulting massive, circular flows of water around the ocean basins (clockwise in the Northern Hemisphere and counterclockwise in the Southern Hemisphere) are referred to as gyres. There are five major gyres in the world's oceans.

This pattern of movement can be seen in the East Australia Current, which becomes South Pacific Current, which then becomes the Peru Current (also known as the Humboldt Current), only to return to east Australia via the South Equatorial Current. We also see this along the northern coast of Japan, where the dumping of North Equatorial Current waters in the western Pacific drives the Kuroshio Current. As the Kuroshio curves to the east, it becomes the North Pacific Current. As the North Pacific Current travels south along the western coast of North America, it becomes the California Current, which completes its circle around the North Pacific as it merges with the North Equatorial Current. The southward-flowing California Current and the northward-flowing Alaska Current are diverted along the western coast of North America.

This basic pattern is repeated on the east coast of North America by the northeastward-flowing Gulf Stream. The Gulf Stream flows north along the U.S. East Coast before curving eastward at 45° N and running toward Northern Europe (carrying out substantial sea-to-air heat transfers at it goes). The Gulf Stream splits as it reaches Europe, with its northern arm turning into the North Atlantic Current (flowing past Ireland and Great Britain) and then the Norwegian Current; its southern arm turns into the Canary Current. The Canary Current flows south along the European coast into the equatorial current where it is reheated it returned to the Americas.

Natural barriers to the dispersal of organisms can be created by powerful currents. For example, the southward flowing California Current is redirected offshore at Point Conception, California, where the shoreline abruptly juts westward; larvae from the north are carried away from habitable space, while larvae from the south are prevented from further northward settlement by the incoming flow. The obstructions created by such currents are a strong factor in the distribution of species.

On the U.S. East Coast, the Gulf Stream runs northward, breaking away from Cape Hatteras, North Carolina to Chesapeake Bay before heading eastward toward the British Isles. Some of these transatlantic currents are surprisingly swift, averaging .01-0.5 meters (0.3-1.5 feet) per second—roughly 1% of the wind speed at 10 meters (30 feet) above the water surface. The interaction of surface currents of different speeds produces long lasting swirls of water. Amazingly, water from surface eddies in the North American East Coast have been found to contain the unique chemical signature of waters from as far away as Gibraltar.

4. Waves and Tides

All waves are characterized by height, length and period. Height is determined by the distance between the highest (i.e. crest) and lowest (i.e. trough) points. The distance between crests is the wavelength. Frequency is determined by the number of crests that pass through a given point in a given amount of time. Water waves that are driven primarily by winds are referred to as forced waves. Those that continue to move along at some pace set by period and wavelength after wind has ceased are referred to as free waves. A series of free waves (or swells) can accumulate. When uninterrupted, swells are known to travel all of the way from the arctic to the Antarctic regions.

In areas where two water wave systems cross, several things may happen. Some may simply pass through unaltered. Two crests may combine to form an even bigger crest. A crest and a trough may cancel each other out. As waves approach a shoreline, they become steeper and less stable. As they fall upon a solid object (e.g. land), they are either reflected, refracted or diffracted. Reflection occurs when a wave, moving perpendicular to a shoreline, bounces back and reverses direction. When striking the shore at an angle, waves are reflected at an angle that is equal to, though 90° off of, the incoming angle. The interference pattern produced in this situation can be extremely complex—even more so when reflecting off of a curved-face feature, where the wave energy can either be increased or reduced depending upon the particular shape of the curve. Refraction occurs where shallow sloping shores slow down and ultimately "break" the waves. Excluding rare cases where waves strike the shore in a perfectly perpendicular manner, different parts of the wave line slow down at different times, causing them to bend as they move into shallower waters. The effects become even more complicated when the coast has large bays or beachheads. Diffraction occurs when waves are bent passing around some impediment or through a narrow passageway, causing wave energy to be dispersed over a wider area. Seiches are standing waves that oscillate (i.e. swing back and forth) in fully or mostly enclosed bodies of water (e.g. aquaria, wave pools, the Black Sea). At one or more points within the basin, water moves in vertical pulses, creating the impression of surges that rise and fall in place. Seiches are generated as a water body is returned by gravity to its resting position after being pushed to one side (e.g. by wind or earthquakes) or being vertically displaced (e.g. by rapid changes of barometric pressure). Oscillation frequencies are generally very stable, regardless of the topography of the basin. Seiches range from scarcely discernable ripples to massively destructive breakers.

The headlands of Point Conception, CA are large enough to divert major oceanic currents. Robert Schwemmer.

Holacanthus bermudensis **in Hampton Bays, NY. On the western sides of ocean basins, tropical species may be found at relatively high latitudes as oceanic gyres transport larvae from the tropics into temperate zones. In the Western Atlantic, the Gulf Stream carries tropical species as far north as Nova Scotia. Todd Gardner.**

While most ocean waves are generated by the force of air movement or seismic activity, the largest of ocean waves—the tides—are considered to be the most important. Tides can be thought of as giant waves so huge that two crests cover the entire ocean. Tidal action is generated by gravitational forces between the Earth, the Sun and the Moon. The length of a tidal cycle is approximately 28 days—the duration of a single lunar revolution around the earth. The Sun's gravitational force on the Earth is far greater (about 177 times) than that of the Moon. However, proximity has a stronger influence on tide-generating force than does mass. The Moon (which is smaller but closer) therefore has a greater influence on tides than the Sun (which is larger but further away). This results in a bulge on the side facing and the side opposite the Moon. These bulges are largest when the Sun and Moon are aligned during new-moon and full-moon phases. Because the planet spins through both bulges every 24 hours and 50 minutes, there typically are two high-tides and two low-tides per day. They occur about an hour later each day, as does the daily overhead passing of the Moon. Pairs of high- and low-tides that are roughly equal are referred to as semidiurnal; those that are unequal are referred to as mixed semidiurnal. The period between changing tides is referred to as a slack tide.

The physical effects of tides are most dramatically manifested along coastal areas, where the constant changes of water level move the shoreline throughout each day. Tidal patterns may be altered by Coriolis deflection, the shape of continents and topography of the seafloor. In the case of a diurnal tide pattern, an area (e.g. the Gulf of California) will experience only one high-tide and one low-tide daily. In some situations, the presence of a large lagoon with narrow passages (such as the Portsmouth and Langstone harbors of southern England) can cause four daily tides (two major and two minor).

The difference in elevation between the lowest low-tide and the highest high-tide is referred to as the tidal range. Most tidal ranges run a couple of meters in height. However, the range can be almost negligible along the mostly enclosed Mediterranean Sea, where exchange with the Atlantic Ocean is restricted by a shallow water barrier (or sill); it can range as widely as 16 meters (52.5 feet) where waters

Exposure during low-tide presents serious challenges for intertidal plants and animals. Medtrails.

stack up in the Bay of Fundy. The gravitational pull of the Sun and Moon combine strength at certain times when the bodies are in line with each other, resulting in especially strong tides. These extreme tides, referred to as spring tides, occur twice monthly (during new and full moons). Tides are weakest when these bodies are at right angles to each other. Referred to as neap tides, these also occur twice monthly (during first quarter and third quarter moons). The effects of extreme high and low tides can be intensified by topography. For example, while the average tidal range throughout Northwestern Europe is between five meters (16 feet) for springs and 3.8 meters (12 ½ feet) for neaps, they seldom reach a meter or two in the semi-enclosed Baltic Sea and may be as great as 14 meters (46 feet) in the face of the Atlantic Ocean at St. Malo, France. Rapid filling and draining of coastal areas during tides can generate strong water movement. Tidal currents bring massive amounts of sediment and other loose material shoreward. These currents change direction with changes in the tidal cycle. Flood currents are caused by rising tides; ebb currents are caused by falling tides. Tidal currents are generally weakest during slack tides.

5. Thermohaline Stratification/Deep Ocean Currents

The Ocean is a stratified structure. Water layers of a uniform density can move together as a single mass. The ocean is basically composed of three such layers: (1) a top layer that encompasses the first 0-550 meters (0-1,800 feet) depth, (2) an intermediate layer that lies from 550-1,500 meters (1,800-4,900 feet) depth and (3) a bottom layer that lies beyond 1,500 meters depth. Surface water density varies somewhat with latitude and season. Water in the uppermost layer generally has a higher temperature and a lower salinity, and so essentially floats on top. Due to wind-driven waves, surface ocean waters are typically fairly well stirred up. Therefore, temperature and salinity remain relatively uniform throughout this mixed layer. If wind speeds are high enough to generate white caps, then the water will likely be very well mixed. Mixed layer depths of around 10 meters (30 feet) are typical. Depending upon the amount of wave energy involved, the depth of the mixed layer can be as much as 1,000 meters (3,200 feet) deep. The pycnocline, the area directly between the mixed surface layer and mostly static deep zone, rapidly increases in density with increasing depth. The shape of the pycnocline is roughly similar to those of the thermocline and halocline. The thermocline rapidly decreases in temperature with increasing depth, whereas the halocline increases in salinity with increasing depth. Temperature and salinity in the deep zone change only slightly with increasing depth.

The physical forces that separate the layers are so strong that the thermocline is affected only where the most powerful mixing occurs. The depth of the thermocline changes throughout the year in temperate seas. Surface waters in temperate regions are heated mostly during the summer, extending to about 50 meters (164 feet). Then, with the approach of winter, surface waters cool and sink into deeper waters, greatly extending the mixed portion; there might not even be a thermocline in polar waters where there is very strong mixing and surface water temperatures are perpetually frigid. The seasonal thermocline, situated in the upper part of the layer, may change over the course of the year. Situated at the lower part of the layer is the permanent thermocline, where temperatures decrease from about 6-10°C (42-50°F) at the bottom of the seasonal thermocline to about 4°C (39°F) at around 1,500 meters depth. Outside of the polar regions, waters below the thermocline rarely drop much below 4°C (39°F). For the most part, the densest (that is, coldest and saltiest) ocean waters rest over the deepest parts of the seafloor at around 4,000 meters (12,800 feet) or greater.

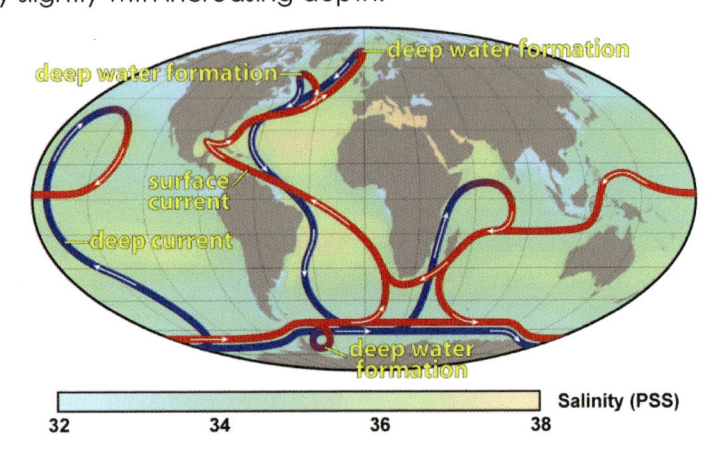

Deep water masses flow over the sea bottom like rivers. Robert Simmon.

Extensive water currents are driven by density gradients. Significant sinkage may take place in certain regions due to the descent of hypersaline surface waters. Surface waters can be denser than underlying waters where there are very low air temperatures. Seawater (unlike freshwater) continually increases in density as its temperature decreases. Surface seawater of a typical salinity freezes at or below −2°C (28°F), a few degrees lower than the freezing point of pure freshwater. Salts extrude from the crystalline structure of the water ice during freezing. Being of a greater density, cooler and saltier water has a tendency to sink below warmer, fresher water. The denser water just beneath the ice sinks to the ocean floor. As it hits the bottom, it flows slowly through any sloping channel in the seafloor. Large, sinking water masses are capable of driving extensive deep water currents. The thermohaline circulation, also referred to as the great ocean conveyor belt, is probably the longest unbroken water current on the planet. Driven primarily by gradients in temperature and salinity, the conveyor belt carries chilled water from higher to lower latitudes at a pace of about 10 centimeters (4 inches) per second; it may take as long as 2,000 years to complete a pass through this circuit.

The layout of the circuit is rather complex. In the arctic basin, cold bottom water streams are pretty much blocked from the Pacific Ocean by the shallowness and narrowness of the Bering Strait. Consequently, most arctic discharges spill into the Atlantic Ocean at a rate of about 100 kilometers (62 miles) per year, mainly into gaps between Greenland and Iceland and between Iceland and Norway. These streams together form what is known as the North Atlantic Deep Water. In the Antarctic, dense seawater (mainly from the Ross and Weddell Seas) flows out at various points into the Pacific, Atlantic and Indian Oceans as the Antarctic Bottom Water. In the Northern Hemisphere, a major area of sinking is located in the Norwegian Sea (where warm Gulf Stream waters meet arctic sea ice) at the North Atlantic Deep Water. In the Southern Hemisphere, a major sink occurs in the Weddell Sea at the Atlantic Bottom Water off of the Antarctic coast. Waters flowing southward from the arctic are slightly less dense than waters flowing northward from the Antarctic; thus, wherever they meet, North Atlantic Deep Water tends to flow over Antarctic Bottom Water.

6. Upwelling

Typically, high-pressure areas develop over Easter Island and the equatorial eastern Pacific, while low-pressure areas develop over Indonesia and the equatorial western Pacific. The resulting trade winds push so much warm equatorial water westward that sea level is about 0.5 meters (20 inches) higher in the western Pacific region. These waters pile up, forming areas with deep thermoclines (known as warm pools). Warm pools are a frequent occurrence between 25° N and 25° S. Because they deepen the thermocline, warm pools form a strong barrier between surface and bottom waters. The opposite occurs in the east. As surface waters move westward, they are displaced by colder waters from the deep (usually 100-200 meters (300-650 feet) depth) in a process referred to as upwelling.

Upwelling occurs mainly along the equator, the eastern boundaries of oceans and throughout the Southern Ocean. Owing to the particular influence of wind and surface water current deflection, upwelling most often occurs along the western coasts of continents. Major seasonal upwelling zones are situated along eastern boundary currents such as the Benguela and Peru Currents. For example, predominant winds along the western South American coast blow northward, generating powerful offshore currents. Deflection of the resulting surface flows to the left pushes water away from the coast, drawing water up from the deep to the nearshore. Similar offshore currents are generated near western coasts in the Northern Hemisphere, where winds travel southward and currents are deflected to the right. From February to August, strong, southeast blowing winds increase the velocity of the California Current surface water flow. Being in the Northern Hemisphere, this flow veers to the right (i.e. away from the coast). As these surface waters drift out westward, they are displaced by cool water from the depths. In some cases, waters from an upwelling zone can drift seaward, forming plumes that may run for over 200 kilometers (120 miles) from the coastline. Certain climatic events (e.g. El Niño) can reverse prevailing wind directions, piling up water in the eastern Pacific Ocean, resulting in warm winters and effectively stalling upwelling.

Upwelling may also result from the interaction of major bottom currents. Due to displacement, as cold polar waters flow toward the equator, warm tropical waters are pushed toward the poles. When bottom currents collide or surface waters part, bottom waters are forced upward towards the surface. An upwelling zone in the Benguela Current (located around 29°-15° S off of the Namibian coast) has typical surface water temperatures of 12-14°C (54-57°F)—far lower than that of the surrounding, characteristically warm tropical waters. A similar situation exists where the Kuroshio and Oyoshio Currents meet. This action brings nutrient-rich waters from the deep to the shallows where they may contribute to algal blooms so thick that the surrounding waters are often of a hazy green color. One such example, the Antarctic Divergence, is an extensive upwelling zone that is formed where the westward flowing Polar Current and the eastward flowing Circumpolar Current meet and diverge at approximately 70° S. Massive coastal upwelling zones near Antarctica are essentially what allows for the great abundance of algae-eating krill, which in turn sustains populations of wide-ranging animals from small fishes to penguins and whales.

Direct mixing by wind or currents is often sufficient to bring nutrients to the surface. For example, as tidal currents roll in and roll out, friction along the seafloor stirs and mixes the deep water, gradually lifting it upward. Tidal mixing occurs mainly near continents, as well as large topographical features such as sea mounts, mid-ocean ridges, etc. Particularly near coastal areas, nutrient levels can increase significantly as sediments are stirred by the crashing waves. Shallowly submerged plateaus off of the eastern coast of Newfoundland receive enough wave action and water flow to keep nutrients perpetually suspended, resulting in one of the most productive fisheries on Earth.

Temperate marine aquaria might undergo continual seasonal changes of light and nutrient availability; this macroalgae-dominated Norwegian rocky intertidal biotope is at the height of its 16-hour daylength "spring bloom." Jon Olav Bjørndal.

II. Biological Geography

1. The Marine Biome

The biosphere includes all living organisms and habitable parts of the planet. A habitat is the sum of all biotic (i.e. biological) and abiotic (i.e. environmental) stuff in a given area. The term biota refers to all of the organisms that occur within a particular habitat. Communities are highly integrated biotic assemblages. The term ecotone is used to denote transitional zones between distinct communities. A subspecies, variety, breed, etc. that is highly adapted to a specific type of environment is referred to as an ecotype. The term ecosystem is used to describe both the physical and biological interactions that take place between closely interconnected habitats. Biotopes describe ecosystems that feature distinct types of geology, climate and biology regardless of where on Earth they occur. The term biome is used to describe a major type of biological system.

The marine biome is vast. Over 97% of all water on Earth is in the oceans, with most of what remains being ice (only 0.05% exists as groundwater and 0.01% as rivers, lakes and water vapor). Approximately 71% of the surface of the Earth is covered with ocean, with 61% of this covering the Northern Hemisphere and 81% covering the Southern Hemisphere. With a total surface area of 581 million square kilometers (361 million square miles) and an average depth of 3.8 kilometers (2.4 miles), we can calculate that the ocean holds a total volume of about 1.4 million cubic kilometers (0.87 million cubic miles)—roughly enough for each of the seven billion people of the world to have a 200 million gallon marine aquarium.

At least by convention, the Ocean is broken into three major parts, the Pacific, Atlantic and Indian Oceans (some give four, to include the Arctic Ocean, or even a fifth, being the Antarctic or Great Southern Ocean). Around 52% of this water resides in the Pacific, with 25% in the Atlantic and 20% in the Indian Oceans. The Pacific Ocean is so large that it has been referred to as the "ocean hemisphere." The Pacific/Atlantic boundary is said to run through the southern tip of Cape Horn, Chile; the Atlantic/Indian Ocean boundary is said to run through Cape Agulhas of South Africa. Smaller bodies of water (i.e. seas) can have even vaguer boundaries.

The biota of the marine biome is extraordinarily rich. Of 34 recognized phyla, 29 include marine species, 14 of which are strictly marine. Though the world's oceans are all interconnected, biogeographers frequently divide the marine biome into several minor biomes, each with its own distinct parts and subparts (e.g. Coastal Biome, Open Ocean Biome, Polar Ocean Biome and so on). Seven distinct latitudinal groups may be recognized, including the (1) Arctic, (2) Cold-Temperate Northern Hemisphere, (3) Warm-Temperate Northern Hemisphere, (4) Tropical, (5) Warm-Temperate Southern Hemisphere, (6) Cold-Temperate Southern Hemisphere and (7) Antarctic regions. Numerous biogeographic regions may be recognized. Burgess (1990) lists no less than fifteen different biogeographic regions (ignoring the polar regions) that are of special interest to the marine aquarist: (1) Temperate Western Atlantic, (2) Tropical Western Atlantic, (3) Tropical Eastern Pacific, (4) Temperate Eastern Pacific, (5) Temperate Western Pacific, (6) Oceania, (7) Tropical Western Pacific, (8) Great Barrier Reef, (9) Northern and Western Indian Ocean, (10) Red Sea, (11) New Zealand, (12) Temperate Australia, (13) Tropical Eastern Atlantic, (14) Temperate Eastern Atlantic and (15) Mediterranean Sea.

Habitat types can be described most basically as either benthic (i.e. seafloor) or pelagic (i.e. open water) environments. The neritic zone encompasses all shallow coastal waters; the oceanic zone encompasses all waters beyond the edges of continents. The benthic zone includes all parts the seafloor extending from the highest shore line to the bottoms of ocean trenches. Benthic habitats may be categorized as either hard-bottom or soft-bottom environments. Organisms that live on or in the seabed are referred to as the benthos.

Benthos that mainly occupy the substrate surface are termed epifaunal, while those that mainly live below it are termed infaunal. Those organisms that live just above or below the water surface (e.g. sea strider (*Halobates* spp.)) are referred to as the neuston. Those that live permanently floating at the very surface (e.g. by-the-wind sailor (*Velella* spp.)) are referred to as pleuston. Larger open water creatures (greater than 20 millimeters), which tend to be much better adapted swimmers, are referred to as nekton. Nektos that are closely associated with the benthic zone are termed demersal. The open water zone can be divided into neritic and oceanic zones. These habitats are populated mainly by small (less than 20 millimeters) and drifting or weakly swimming organisms that are referred to as the plankton. Benthic and nektonic species may undergo a planktonic larval stage.

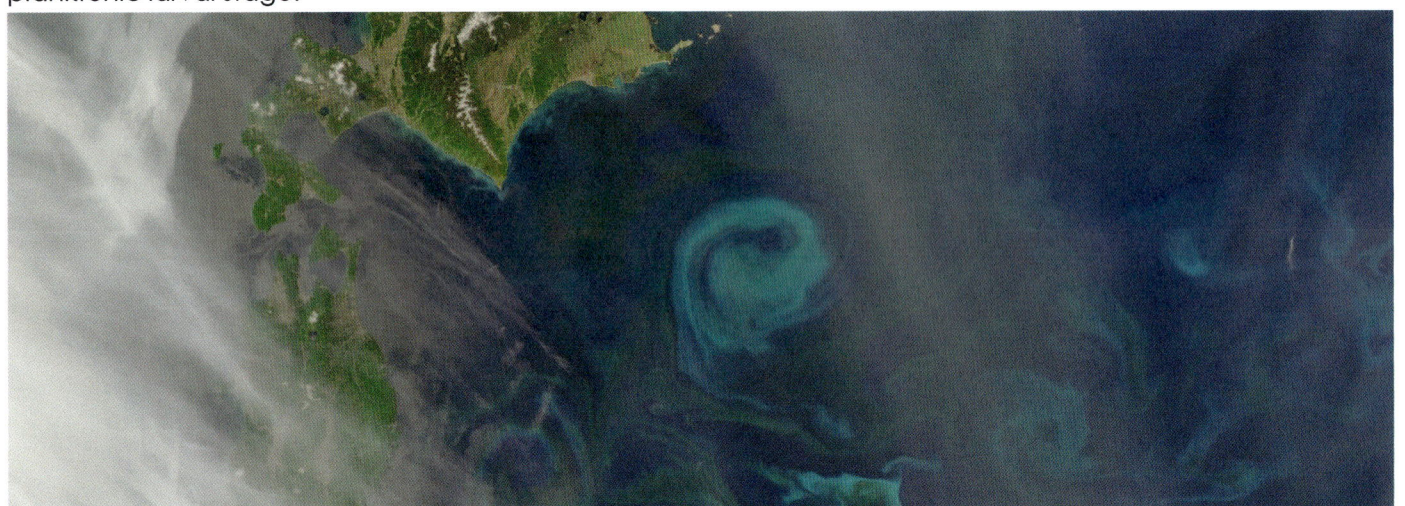

Phytoplankton concentrates along an eddy caused by a collision of the Oyashio and Kuroshio Currents. Norman Kuring.

Some use the term plankton to describe all open-water organisms that lack a means to swim against currents and tides. Some include in this group all non-swimmers from free-living viruses to the largest of jellyfish. They are most typically categorized as either phytoplankton (i.e. tiny plants) or zooplankton (i.e. tiny animals). Planktonic forms can be categorized rather roughly by size and taxonomy into (1) the bacterioplankton, (2) the phytoplankton, (3) the zooplankton and (4) the metazooplankton. The term nanoplankton refers to those that are 2.0-20 micrometers in size (usually protozooplankton such as ciliates, foraminiferans and radiolarians); the term ultraplankton is used for those <2.0 micrometers (usually bacterioplankton). There are two types of bacterioplankton: free-living varieties that tend to be less than one micrometer in size and those that attach to particles of organic matter and tend to be larger than one micrometer. The phytoplankton are a diverse group of cyanobacteria and single-celled algae (2-200 micrometers) that use light-sensitive pigments to capture solar energy.

One of the most important properties of water is its transparency. There is a finite distance through which sunlight can penetrate seawater. Around 3.5% of light is attenuated per meter depth in clear water. In clear water, 50% of sunlight is absorbed in the first 12 meters (39 feet) of depth; in murkier waters it is more like seven meters (23 feet). Most infrared solar energy is absorbed in the very first meter of depth. Visible light may penetrate several hundred meters into clear water. That notwithstanding, some wavelengths of visible light are more readily absorbed than others; red (low-frequency) light is very quickly absorbed with only 1% remaining at 10 meters (32 feet) depth, while blue (high-frequency) light is less readily absorbed with 1% remaining at 150 meters (492 feet) depth (hence the preponderance of blue light at certain depths). From above the surface, deep, clear ocean waters appear blue because they absorb more long-wavelength light; mostly shorter blue wavelengths are scattered and reflected back. As sunlight cannot penetrate water depths greater than 1,000 meters (3,280 feet), deeper waters are darker and colder—often less than 4°C (39°F).

Light intensity decreases exponentially with increasing water depth. This behavior can be described by the equation:

$$I(d) = I(0)e^{-kd}$$

where light intensity at depth d, I(d) equals the intensity of light at the water surface times the value e (base of natural logarithms, ≈2.718) raised to the power -kd (k is an extinction coefficient, k=0.035 per meter). In clear conditions, 10% of sunlight that strikes the ocean surface reaches 50 meters (160 feet) of depth; only 1% reaches 100 meters (350 feet) of depth. The depth at which 1% of surface light remains is generally considered to be the transition between two major photic zones. The epipelagic zone includes the first 200 meters (660 feet) of depth. It is only in the euphotic (or sunlight) zone that light intensity is sufficient for photosynthesis to take place. The depth at which light intensity is just strong enough to support plant life is referred to as the compensation depth. This sunlit zone is situated in the shallowest parts, accounting for just 2.5% of ocean waters, with a vast aphotic (or dark) zone beneath it. Some use the term disphotic zone (or twilight zone) to describe the dim stretch between the euphotic and aphotic zones.

With over 84% of its waters being deeper than 2,000 meters (6,000 feet), around 97.5% of the ocean is pitch dark. The mesopelagic zone is a rather barren seascape extending some 200-1,000 meters (660-3,300 feet). The bathyal zone (or midnight zone) includes a part of the pelagic zone at a depth of 1,000-4,000 meters (3,300-13,000 feet). The abyssopelagic (lower midnight) extends from 4,000 meters (13,000 feet) to the bottom of the ocean basin. The greatest depths are in the oceanic trenches of the hadal zone; the deepest part yet discovered is 10,911 meters (35,814 feet). Exploration of the dark, deep sea environment (e.g. the 2016 *Okeanos Explorer* expeditions) continues to reveal more and more about its mysterious inhabitants.

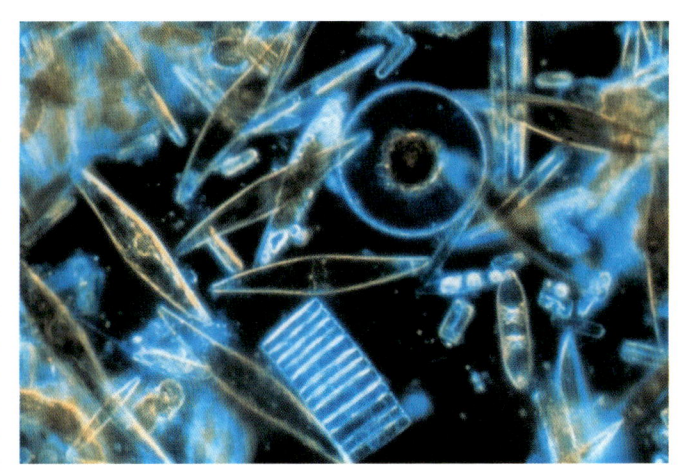

Diatoms are the dominant phytoplankter in shallow temperate waters. Prof. Gordon T. Taylor.

Marine environments are greatly influenced by water depth and distance from the shore. Water pressure increases by one atmosphere with every 10 meters of depth. The relationship between a particular depth and the weight of the overlying waters is referred to as hydrostatic pressure. The volume of a compressed gas is inversely proportional to the absolute pressure. A particular volume of gas will be compressed in seawater to half of its volume at 10 meters (2 bar), a third at 20 meters (3 bar), a quarter at 30 meters (4 bar), etc. Though the bodily tissues of marine organisms are composed mainly of solids and liquids that are pretty much incompressible by water, many fishes and cephalopods rely on bodily gasses (typically contained in special body cavities) to control buoyancy and internal pressure. These organs must be capable of adjusting buoyancy with changes in depth. During very rapid ascents, expanding gasses can rupture the organ. This type of injury can often be observed among wild-caught deep-water species that are brought too quickly to the water surface.

2. Coastal Habitats

Coastal (or littoral) environments lie in a transitional zone that encompasses everything from soggy puddles on the high shore down to waters just deep enough (around 60 meters (200 feet)) that storm waves can unsettle the seafloor. There are conceivably as many types of coasts as there are coasts; each has its own unique physical environment and ecosystem. The coastline serves as a boundary between the terrestrial and marine realms. Coastlines are largely formed by geological, climatic and even biological processes. The shoreline is a narrower strip that shifts with the tides. Coastal terrain is continually built up and wore down through the action of wind, rain, rivers, currents and waves. Where the depth of the wind-mixed surface layer exceeds the depth of the seafloor, soft bottoms can be disturbed. Substrates composed of unconsolidated sediments are regularly suspended and relocated. The softer the material the land mass is formed from and the farther it stretches into the ocean, the higher the rate of erosion. The depth at which these currents first reach the bottom serves as the boundary between nearshore and offshore waters.

Waves almost always approach the shoreline at some angle. This concentrates their force at protruding bluffs and weakens it in sheltered coves and harbors. Land features furthest out into the ocean are called headlands. These features refract ocean waves, which reduces water velocity between them and the shore, leading to the formation of landforms called tombolos. The resultingly uneven rates of erosion produce features such as caves, stacks and arches. Wave strength is stronger at headlands than in bays. Consequently, headlands are subjected to heavy erosion while bays tend to accumulate sediments. This somewhat balancing pattern of erosion tends to straighten out coastlines over time.

Beaches develop along coastal shores where wind and water action deposit and reworks sediments. The effects of waves, tides and longshore currents on benthic habitats are most evident over these landforms. A beach may be composed of boulders, cobbles, gravel, sand or mud. Mudflats form in areas of low wave action, whereas cobble beaches form where there is strong wave action. Sandy or muddy bottoms tend to be flat whereas cobble-bottom environments tend to be steep. Often, coarser particles are deposited higher on the beach while finer and finer grades are to found further and further from shore. Berms may be present along the edges of the backshore and foreshore, running parallel to the shoreline. There may be two berms during summer months. There is a winter berm (which is the largest) that is built up from materials deposited by waves pushed onto the beach during winter storms; the lower, summer, berm is typically eroded by strong wave action during the winter months. The steeply sloping seaward side of each berm is referred to as a beach scarp. A flattened area referred to as a low-tide terrace may be present just below the average low-tide level. A beach's shape and composition determines the type of organisms that can reside there. Due to the strong—even violent—water movement encountered there, cobble bottoms are much more hostile to higher life forms.

Estuaries are fully or partially enclosed water bodies (e.g. bays) in which seawater is significantly diluted by freshwater from rivers and run-off. Estuarine environments typically take the form of shallow bays, but they may also be formed from deep fjords. Many inlets, sounds and gulfs may be referred to as estuaries on the basis of their position and freshwater input. Though protected from the rough coastal waters, estuaries can be stressful environments. Whereas daily temperature changes in open ocean waters are usually less than 0.3 degrees C (0.5 degrees F), daily temperatures may vary in these enclosed bodies by as much as 3.0 degrees C (5.4 degrees F). Moreover, a salinity gradient is established from the estuary head (where it communicates with the river) to the mouth (where it communicates with the ocean). As it travels downstream, water salinity changes from fresh to brackish to moderately salty (up to 18 ppt); salinity abruptly increases near the lower parts (from 18 ppt to 35 ppt). Being of a lesser density, freshwater from rivers floats above the saltier waters of the estuary. Often, this results in a bidirectional flow, where river water flows over the surface toward the sea while on the bottom seawater moves inland (many organisms follow this pattern of circulation to move in and out of the estuary). A salt wedge may form where a large freshwater surface layer drives incoming seawater further inland. If the freshwater input is very high, salinity will be significantly lower inland; however, if input is very low and evaporation rates are high, salinity may be lower seaward, resulting in what is referred to as a reverse estuary. In steep, narrow estuaries (where deep-water exchange is limited), bottom waters may be both very salty and stagnant. Mixing increases with increasing tidal range. Partially mixed conditions are most common. Partially mixed estuaries develop where (1) freshwater input is moderate and (2) there is still an appreciable surface-to-bottom gradient in salinity.

The New Zealand longfin eel migrates through estuaries as part of its life cycle. Gusmonkeyboy.

Each estuary has its own freshwater input and tidal range. The average period of time that a confined area is flooded is referred to as the residence time. Residence times may be of different lengths at different locations in the same body of water. For example, in Puget Sound, the residence time of the main basin is about two months, though it is something like 6-12 months in some remote sections. Reflection of tides is restricted in confined bays, increasing the difference between high- and low-tides at the head of the bay (e.g. Bay of Fundy). The buildup can result in a spilling wave front that travels up a river or bay at a speed of up to 40 kilometers (25 miles) per hour. This condition, known as a tidal bore, occurs mainly over shallow river mouths and bays. Typical tidal bores are usually about a meter in height, but may exceed 8 meters (26 feet).

Coastal environments may be divided into three distinct zones: (1) the supralittoral zone (or splash zone), (2) the eulittoral zone (or intertidal zone) and (3) the sublittoral zone (or subtidal zone). Only infrequently covered with water, the splash zone is wetted by nothing more than sea spray and rainfall. These shoreline environments include areas just above the high-tide mark, such as strandlines, sand dunes, sea cliffs and high beaches. Water that has been driven onto a beach by waves is known as swash. Substrates can be highly unstable due to the action of swash and backswash. But far more complex cycles of submergence and air exposure occur in intertidal zones, where land and sea overlap. Distinguished by substrate composition, there are four basic types of intertidal habitat: (1) rocky shores, (2) sandy shores, (3) muddy shores and (4) salt marshes.

Life on the high seashore has both advantages and disadvantages for a Waratah anemone. Gary Houston.

Deep-dwelling fishes must contend with increased hydrostatic pressure and reduced visibility. James Hoehlein.

At least in many respects, conditions are far more stable just beyond the lower reaches of the tides. Never exposed to air, the subtidal zone is defined as the area extending from the lowest low-tide to the deepest bottoms affected by wave action. It encompasses the shallowest parts of the continuously submerged, gently sloping fringe of a continent known as a continental shelf. The upper part of the subtidal zone, an algae-dominated area (except on soft bottoms) usually situated at around 5 meters (16 feet) below the low water mark, is referred to as the infralittoral zone. Substrate composition and slope greatly affect infralittoral species composition. Horizontal or slightly sloped substrata are favored by macroalgae while steep, rocky cliffs are favored by sessile animals. The epifaunal invertebrate-dominated area just beyond an infralittoral algal bed is referred to as the circalittoral zone.

Continental shelves extend seaward from the lowest low-tide mark to the edge of the continental mass itself. The average width of the shelf is 78 kilometers (48 miles). In some cases the shelf might end just offshore and in others extend over 200 kilometers (124 miles) from the shoreline. The shelf is gently sloping at a grade of approximately 1:50 (1°). The average depth of water over the continental shelf is 132 meters (430 feet). The open waters above this stretch make up the neritic zone. A transitional zone at the seaward side of the shelf (or shelf front) marks a barrier between the mixed and stratified masses of water. The front can be dissipated to some extent in the midlatitudes during fall and winter surface cooling. Sinks can develop over the edge of the shelf when cold waters drop from its precipice into the deep (e.g. the Irish Sea). Just below the outermost edge of the continental shelf (or the shelf-slope break), usually at 100-200 meters (328-656 feet) of depth, lies the continental slope. The continental slope is steep, with a grade of approximately 1:20 (2.9°). The foot of the slope, the continental rise, is characterized by a somewhat lower gradient. At the bottom of the rise (roughly four kilometers (2.5 miles) below sea level), the seafloor flattens out for a few more kilometers into a vast abyssal plain. This flatness is interrupted only by sparse seamounts or mid-ocean ridges. The continental margin, an area that includes the shelf, slope and rise, claims about 25% of the seafloor. Though accounting for only 0.15% of the ocean by volume, continental shelf habitats are among the most biologically productive.

The biological communities of the continental shelf and intertidal zone are extraordinarily diverse. These coastal habitats vary greatly with differences of water depth, substrate type, offshore distance or even time of year.

3. Major Regional Biotopes

Just as tropical seas are said to have the greatest biodiversity of all marine biomes, the temperate seas might be regarded as having the greatest diversity of habitat types. Temperate coastal areas are particularly rich in distinct habitats. These disparate environments, as well as the cohorts of organisms that reside therein, change rapidly with increasing water depth.

Though exposed to saltwater only by spring tides and crashing waves, even the uppermost reaches of the supralittoral fringe are subject to the powerful influence of the ocean. The fringe may be divided into two distinct zones: (1) the higher parts, which are dominated by terrestrial flora (salt-tolerant higher plants, certain lichens, mosses, etc.) and the lower parts, which are dominated by other lichens (e.g. *Verrucaria*) and cyanobacteria, which impart a dark band along the high-tide line. In temperate regions, annual algae appear during the winter months, adding a greenish or brownish hue. Perennial algae may also appear, though only in those areas with the highest humidity and strongest wave action. Glassworts and marsh grasses may dominate along the fringe, assembled in patches according to salt tolerance. A wide-ranging assemblage of coastal fauna occur at the fringe, including periwinkle snails (*Littorina* spp.), amphipods (e.g. *Ligia* and *Megaligia* spp.), grapsid crabs (*Grapsus* spp.) and hermit crabs (e.g. *Calcinus* spp.) as well as various insects, spiders, small mammals and birds. Supralittoral sea cliffs are inhabited by many creatures, but are usually most heavily populated by seabirds for their excellent nesting sites. These birds affect the area greatly by feeding on intertidal organisms and by fertilizing the surrounding rocks and waters with their excrement. Sand dunes and sand banks often contain little or no marine life; only resilient little animals such as the ghost crab (*Ocypode quadrata*) and a few tough, wind-tolerant plants such as sea sandwort (*Honkenya* spp.) and dune lichen (*Cladonia* spp.) can survive here. A slender band of debris along a beach (or strandline) is formed at or just above the high tide mark. The position of the strandline on the beach is highest after strong storms or spring equinox tides. This tangled mess may include anything from driftwood, pieces of seaweed (or wrack), egg masses, shell hash, feathers, human trash, etc. The sand hopper (*Talitrus saltitor*) as well as many terrestrial insects scavenge intensely upon any organic matter deposited here. Specially adapted organisms such as the thrift (*Armeria maritima*), sea campion (*Silene maritima*) and encrusting black lichen (*Verrucaria maura*) live among the sea sprayed stones; even a few barnacles might venture into the wetter parts of this area.

Intertidal environments are subjected to many extremes while exposed to air during low-tide. They may freeze or be baked in the direct sunlight; intertidal water temperatures can wander as much as 22 degrees C (40 degrees F) in as little as 12 hours. Waves might repeatedly crash into them with the force of a hurricane. They may dry out (though the substrate never dries completely). The pool waters may quickly turn anoxic. Salinity may fluctuate wildly; it can either plummet with the influx of rainwater or spike where rapid evaporation occurs. Biological adaptations to these stressors frequently depend upon the type of substrate that is present.

Rocky shores are characterized by a substrate composed mainly of boulders, cobbles and gravels of a large particle size; in some cases, they are a solid, unbroken mass of stone. Rocky shores are formed where winds and waves have removed all soft sediments, more or less leaving only bare, heavy stone behind. Many different types of stone can be found here, ranging from very hard types such as granite to softer types such as limestone and sandstone. Pockets in the solid stone trap receding waters during low-tides. Tide pools range in depth from a few centimeters to a few meters. The largest are usually found at the bottom of the shore. Tide pools protect small animals such as snails and hermit crabs that find themselves trapped on higher parts of the shore when waters are down. The most mobile creatures can wander from pool to pool at will. Deeper, cooler pools may even provide sufficient cover for sessile invertebrates such as sponges and serpulid worms. Constantly disturbed by wave action, gravel and shingle beaches are home to only a few highly adapted plants and animals. Certainly they are the least stable of rocky shore environments, with pebbles and small cobbles 2.0-200 millimeters (0.078740-7.8740 inches).

Patches of hard and soft substrata are often found mingled together. Kenneth Wingerter.

Isocradactis magna **prefers a mix of rocky and gravelly materials. Graham Bould.**

Sandy shores are characterized by a substrate composed mainly of silica-based minerals of a particle size from 0.063-2.0 millimeters (0.024803–0.078740 inches) in diameter. Sandy shores develop over gentler slopes where water movement is of just the right strength that sand is deposited while mud and silt is carried away. Particularly at low-tide, sandy shores may appear to be completely devoid of higher lifeforms. However, there are usually a few creatures to be found just below the surface. Predators (shrimps, crabs, small flatfish, etc.) move in during high tides to feed on small invertebrates. Myriad microorganisms (bacteria, protozoa, microalgae, etc.) live on or between the individual grains of sand. On the other hand, macroalgae and higher plants are mainly absent on these ever-shifting substrates.

Muddy shores are characterized by a substrate composed mainly of a mix of organic silts and clay particles from 0.063 down to as little as 0.002 millimeters (0.000078740-0.0024803 inches) in diameter. Muddy shores host greater biological diversity and abundance than sandy shores, as they are capable of accumulating greater stores of organic particulates and dissolved nutrients. *Tubifex* spp. worms can be very abundant in these rich sediments. Grazers such as the mud snail (*Hydrobia ulvae*) can reach huge densities on estuarine mudflat surfaces. Like sandy shores, this soft bottom environment provides habitat for burrowing animals (many prefer a mixture of sand and mud, which allows for the most stable burrow walls). Most burrowing sea anemones prefer a hard surface to attach to (e.g. buried stones) as well as some rubble with which they may cloak themselves.

Wetlands are areas of poor drainage which are occasionally or permanently covered by water. Salt marshes form in wetlands (e.g. the margins of muddy shores) that retain seawater during high-tides. Salt marshes are most often found near mudflats with very fine, primarily organic sediments at latitudes of around 65° N and S. These environments are replaced by mangrove swamps in lower latitudes; only in a few areas (e.g. the U.S. Gulf region, southeast Australia) do mangroves and salt marsh grasses mingle. The greatest diversity of true marine plants occurs in salt marshes; many salt-tolerant grasses, sedges and rushes as well as the leadworts (Plumbaginaceae) can be found in great abundance here. With an influx of nutrients from both land and sea, salt marshes contain some of the highest biomass per unit area than most other marine ecosystems. Marsh grasses dominate where silt builds up along the top of the tidal range. Salt meadow cordgrass (*Spartina alterniflora*) can form dense, erosion-resistant peat beds. By retaining sediments, these plants help to enrich the developing soil. The substrates in *Spartina*-dominated marshes are held together by the grasses' roots, which help to stabilize the shore bottoms. Additionally, cordgrass roots and stems allow for the attachment of mussels, which further stabilizes the shores. As canopy-forming plant species begin to take hold there, their shade cools the understory, thereby reducing evaporation and lowering salinity, which allows for an even higher level of plant diversity.

Salt meadow cordgrass is adapted to withstand regular tidal inundation. USDA-NRCS PLANTS Database.

Seagrass meadows typically occur on soft bottoms from the low-tide mark to around 50 meters (165 feet) depth. Seagrasses prefer sheltered, well-lit areas. They can be found in both tropical and temperate, but not polar, regions. There are about 50 species of seagrass (most of which are tropical). Tropical and temperate seagrasses are rather different from one another and are well separated geographically. In temperate latitudes, the dominant type of seagrass is eelgrass (*Zostera* spp.). Many species of macroalgae and microalgae grow on the seagrass blades, adding complexity to the meadow structure. Seagrasses create vital habitat for numerous animal species. They provide hiding space for small animals such as snails, polychaete worms, isopods, shrimps and juvenile fish. They provide an attachment site for small invertebrates such as hydrozoans, bryozoans, tunicates and small sponges. Larger animals may visit the meadow to feed or to spawn (seagrass habitats are important marine fish and shellfish nurseries).

Macroalgal beds typically occur on hard bottoms from the low-tide mark to around 20-40 meters (65-120 feet) depth. Most macroalgal kelp beds can be seen well from the shore only during low spring tides. Where the grade of the shelf slope is slight, they can extend 5-10 kilometers (3-6 miles) offshore. As kelps prefer cool waters (5-15°C (41-59°F)), they are restricted mainly to temperate environments from the subpolar regions to the 20° N/S summer isotherms. Although 25% of continental shelves lie in the polar regions, kelp beds are modest or

A *Posidonia* meadow stabilizes sediments along the Spanish coast. Nanosanchez.

nonexistent at the highest latitudes due to regular shading and scouring by ice. Kelps are most abundant near upwelling zones in the western Pacific Ocean near China and Japan, the North and South American west coasts, the seaboards of eastern Canada, southern Greenland, Northern Europe, New Zealand, South Africa, southern Australia and the Falkland Islands. Their range only extends into subtropical regions that receive currents from deeper, cooler waters (e.g. the California, Peru and Benguela Currents). Structures formed from larger kelp types may be termed kelp forests (rather than beds), as they develop a tall surface canopy. Canopies of giant kelps such as *Macrocystis pyrifera*, *Neurocystis leutkeana* or *Ecklonia maxima* can tower 5-20 meters (16-65 feet) over the seafloor, while mature beds of smaller kelps such as *Laminaria* and *Agarum* might be less than a meter tall. Some kelps can reach lengths of 50 meters (165 feet) and grow so thickly that they (much like seagrasses) create habitat for many small creatures. Over 300 invertebrate species and 125 fish species were found to be closely associated with a single forest off of the California coast. The complex fabric of kelp forests is disturbed from time to time by surges related to especially strong winter storms. Many kelps (e.g. *Laminaria* spp.) are strongly seasonal in their patterns of growth, growing aggressively during the winter and spring months, only to begin a period of decline around midsummer. Some types may nearly completely die off before the cycle starts anew. Though temperate macroalgal beds are dominated by kelps, sometimes red or green algae will be quite prevalent. Vast, shallow bay bottoms in the Gulf of California develop covers of the green alga *Caulerpa sertularoides* that may reach a thickness of over 10 centimeters (4 inches).

The abundance of erect macroalgae decreases, while that of sessile invertebrate species increases, on gently sloping substrata with increasing depth. This depth emergent property is more conspicuous in temperate than in tropical regions, where large kelps are all but absent. By strict definition, a reef is a large, solid, shallowly submerged mass. So, it might follow that coral reefs are rocky masses that are covered with corals. Corals occur in nearly every reach of the ocean. Still, for many of us, the term coral reef conjures images of clement seas teeming with so-called reef-building, zooxanthellate (that is, photosynthetic) corals. Yet, those corals are restricted to tropical and warm subtropical

Tall kelps (such as these *Macrocystis* sp.) greatly increase habitat complexity. NOAA.

regions to around 35° N and S. Strong sunlight, very clear waters and water temperatures of 22°-27°C (72°-80°F) are necessary for full stony coral reef development. Outside of this narrow zone, nearly all corals are azooxanthellate. It is thought that overgrowth by algae, rather than the direct influence of the cool waters, is primarily responsible for the lack of extensive coral growth in shallow midlatitude waters. But large colonies of azooxanthellate corals (along with countless sponges, bryozoans, ascidians, brachiopods, etc.) are often found at the shelf-slope break, which provides an excellent reef structure. Organic particulates that rain down from the surface, as well as nutrient-rich waters upwelled along the slope, bring additional food sources. Seaward-flowing currents deliver organic sediments from terrestrial environments to rich communities of filter-feeding epifauna on infralittoral ledges.

Corallium rubrum and *Parazoanthus axinellae* **dominate this Mediterranean reef scene. Parent Géry.**

Algae are responsible for most marine photosynthesis. Algal primary production is often very high in waters near the continents, where runoff and upwelling contribute to elevated nutrient levels. Some of the most fertile habitats are found in the open waters over continental shelves. These waters support enough phytoplankton to in turn support large assemblages of animals. The highest concentration of nutrients (and thus plankton) over the shelf is found where currents collide (e.g. the point of contact between the Labrador Current and the Gulf Stream). Massive standing crops of plankton play an integral role in the transport of nutrients between all marine ecosystems. The largest (albeit patchiest) populations of plankton are found in coastal and nearshore areas where light conditions and nutrient availability are optimal. Being as most marine life is concentrated in the shallows, nutrients there can be depleted rather quickly. In tropical regions, where perpetually warm surface layers hinder nutrient exchange with cooler bottom waters, planktonic communities are (despite high light levels) severely nutrient-limited. Coincidentally, in polar regions, where annual solar radiation is low, they are (despite strong mixing/high nutrient availability) severely light-limited. In temperate regions, however, there is just enough sunlight and there are just enough nutrients to support rich plankton blooms. Much of the ocean is fairly well stratified in the mid-latitudes during the summer months. During the autumn months at 45°-50° N and S, cooling surface waters begin to erase the thermocline. Then, winter storm waves mix the water mass deeply. Massive blooms occur as day lengths begin to increase in the spring. This persists until early summer, when the thermocline develops anew. Unusually cold, stormy weather conditions can cause a second (albeit smaller) bloom in early autumn if they disrupt the thermocline before the photoperiod decreases too much. Periods of

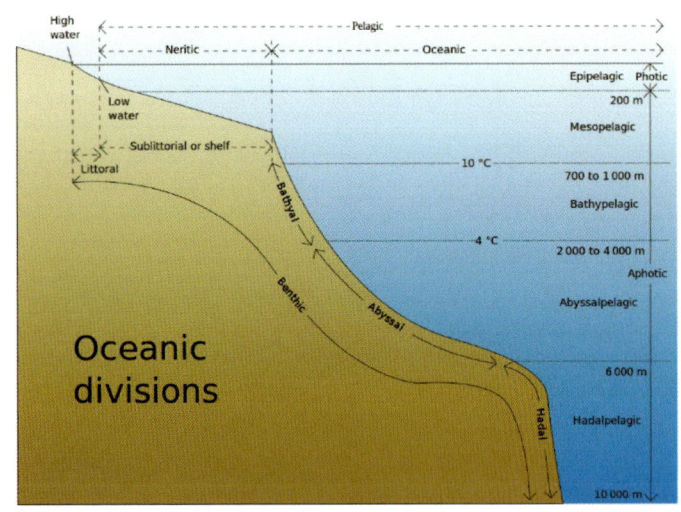

The neritic zone covers only a relatively small, shallow portion of the marine biome. Chris huh.

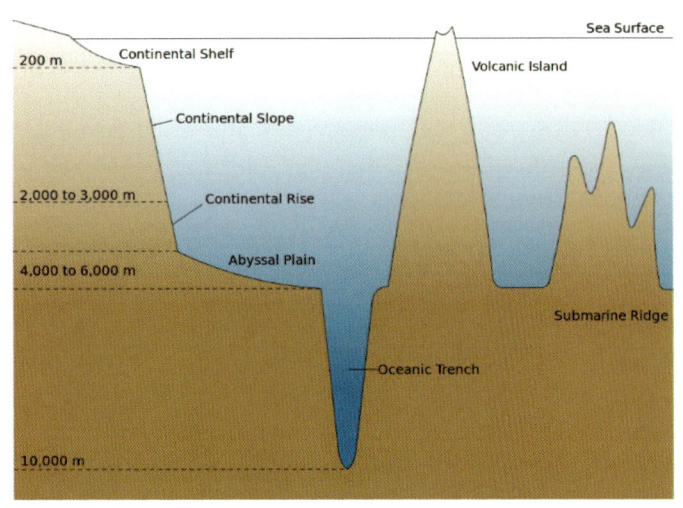

While much of the seafloor is flat, continental margins and ocean basins can be quite irregular topographically. Chris huh.

peak phytoplankton production are followed by periods of peak zooplankton production. These swings in population size are moderated somewhat where overwintering zooplankton limit the size of early spring blooms (e.g. the North Pacific Ocean). In the English Channel, zooplankton biomass often exceeds that of phytoplankton owing to a small but highly productive standing crop of microalgae.

Under the direction of daily light cycles, many plankton undertake a daily vertical migration through the water column. Generally, they descend into the deep during daylight hours and ascend to the surface as dusk sets in. They rise to the surface during outgoing tides, where they remain for several hours until the next incoming tide. Though the capacity of some of these creatures for horizontal movement may be limited, they may be capable of extraordinary vertical movement. Smaller plankters might move vertically at a pace of about 400 meters (1,300 feet) per day; larger zooplankton may be capable of reaching a pace of over 1,000 meters (3,300 feet) per day. A phytoplankter might move through different depths due to wave action and surface currents, constantly changing its access to light. Thus, it is the *average* resident depth that is of most consequence with respect to photosynthesis. The average depth at which a plant receives just enough light exposure to survive, termed the critical depth, may actually extend far below the compensation depth. Phytoplankton are usually most abundant at a depth of around three meters (nine feet). Things get a bit more complicated when the waters are choppy and sunlight is strong enough at the surface to cause harm.

When injured, certain phytoplankton species release a chemical precursor to dimethyl sulfide (DMS). Other organisms convert the compound to DMS, which may then be sent airborne via sea spray. This accelerates cloud formation, which reduces the amount of sunlight reaching the ocean surface. DMS is largely responsible for that "sea smell" as well as reddish sunsets.

III. Marine Ecology
1. Food Chains/Food Webs

All living organisms need a source of fixed carbon to survive, grow and reproduce. Based upon their sources of carbon and energy, species are categorized as (1) chemoautotrophic, (2) photoautotrophic, (3) chemoheterotrophic or (4) photoheterotrophic. Every form of life belongs to one of these four basic groups. Autotrophs synthesize organic substances from inorganic substances. For this reason they are oftentimes referred to as primary producers. Chemoautotrophs obtain energy from inorganic substances whereas photoautotrophs obtain energy from light. Heterotrophs cannot synthesize organic substances from inorganic substances and so obtain them from autotrophs or other heterotrophs. For this reason they are oftentimes referred to as consumers. Chemoheterotrophs obtain energy from organic substances whereas photoheterotrophs obtain energy from light.

Based upon its primary food source, every lifeform is assigned to a particular trophic level. Food energy is transferred from one trophic level to the next along a food chain. Primary producers form the base of every food chain. Primary consumers, the herbivores, make up a second class. A third class, the tertiary consumers, is made up of carnivores. First-level carnivores are made up of animals that feed on herbivores. Top carnivores are at the end of every food chain (to a 6th level or higher). Decomposers and detritivores feed on non-living plant or animal material and waste products. Energy flow is a one-way process; by the end of the food chain, this energy has been entirely lost as heat and is not recoverable. In actual fact, biological processes are quite inefficient. Being as only about 10% of the energy consumed is passed from one trophic level to the next, food chains are cut rather short. This inefficiency (referred to as *trophic inefficiency*, E) is sometimes illustrated using the Trophic Pyramid of Energy. The first trophic level is represented by the base of the pyramid with top-level predators at its tip. The nature of the energy transfer determines the maximum population size and maximum total biomass of each consumer species along the food chain. For example, phytoplankton of the continental shelf are larger than they are elsewhere, leading to an overall greater energy flow to local predatory fish species. Animals that occupy higher trophic levels must consume much more prey to meet their energy needs. This requires that individuals control larger areas, resulting in much smaller populations.

An ecosystem can support only a limited number of top-level carnivores. Kristin Riser.

As the flow of carbon and energy in the real, natural setting is usually far more complex than those modeled in food chains, the term food web may be more appropriate. Food web models account for indirect interaction between trophic levels such as trophic cascades. Trophic cascades occur when an organism limits the abundance or alters the behavior of another organism in such a way that it promotes the abundance of organisms in an unconnected trophic level. Cascades may be described as either top-down (i.e. consumer-driven) or as bottom-up (i.e. producer-driven). In an example of a consumer-driven cascade, overfishing has altered coastal habitats in Maine by shifting the balance from larger to smaller predatory fish species (e.g. sculpins, cunners and shannies). An especially dramatic example of a trophic cascade can be observed where sea urchins are preyed on by sea otters. By controlling the insatiably herbivorous sea urchins, sea otters help to preserve lush kelp forests. Where otters have been heavily exploited by the fur trade, kelps were quickly reduced into what are known as sea urchin barrens. An apex predator can affect a handful of lower trophic levels. For example, by preying heavily on herring, cod indirectly reduce predatory pressure on its prey's prey, zooplankton, which in turn flourishes and increases grazing pressure on phytoplankton. The definitive effect of this wide reaching cascade is strong enough that changes in cod populations can actually impact water clarity.

2. Primary Production

Essentially, primary production involves the fixation of carbon. Carbon fixation reactions "fix" CO_2 to organic molecular precursors. In the most rigid terms, organic compounds are substances that contain carbon atoms that are covalently bonded to one another. By this definition, biomolecules that contain only a single carbon atom (such as calcium carbonate) are to be considered inorganic. Primary production is limited by (1) the availability of light/chemical energy and (2) the producer's own capacity for carbon fixation. The second of these two factors is determined by (1) the size of the standing crop and (2) the organism's intrinsic rate of growth. Thus, a small, flourishing standing crop can in some cases fix carbon at the same rate as a larger, but slow-growing, population.

Chemoautotrophic bacteria are most often found where sunlight is very weak or absent, typically using hydrogen sulfide (H_2S) as a source of energy by oxidizing sulfur to convert it into its elemental form (S) or sulfate (SO_4^{2-}). Rather than being completely lost as heat, some of this energy is directed to carbon fixation. While extremely important in certain marginal environments, chemosynthesis contributes relatively little to annual global productivity. On the other hand, life on Earth as we know it cannot exist without photosynthesis. Photosynthesis is carried out through the reaction of CO_2 with hydrogen from water to yield the carbohydrate glucose ($C_6H_{12}O_6$). An endless variety of more complex carbohydrates and other organic substances may then be formed from the basic structure of simple carbohydrates such as glucose. CO_2 is considered to be a reactant rather than a nutrient. CO_2 is highly soluble in water (about 60 times more concentrated in seawater than in the atmosphere). Once solvated, the gas reacts with water to first form carbonic acid (H_2CO_3), which quickly dissociates into a bicarbonate ion (HCO_3^-) and a hydrogen ion (H^+). This process can be expressed by the equation:

$$CO_2 + H_2O \leftrightarrow H_2CO_3 \leftrightarrow H^+ + HCO_3$$

As we can see from the double-headed arrows, the reaction can reverse itself. The solubility of CO_2 shifts with changes under different physical and chemical conditions. The enzyme anhydrase, which essentially removes water from bicarbonate to release CO_2, is present in the cell walls of most marine autotrophs. Once sequestered by the cell, CO_2 is further processed (i.e. its carbon is fixed) in membranous intracellular structures called plastids. Chloroplasts (which likely evolved from ancient photoautotrophic bacteria) are a feature of all algae and higher plants. These structures are generally disc-shaped with a highly folded double membrane. In the fluid-filled space within the inner membrane, the stroma, is an interconnected series of flat sacs called thylakoids that are arranged in stacks called grana. Certain enzymes in the stroma catalyze the reactions that convert CO_2 into a glucose precursor in the dark reactions (i.e. those that can occur in the absence of light).

In a process called the light reactions, photosynthetic pigments use energy emitted by photons to split H_2O. Light energy absorbed by photopigments is diverted for use in three processes. Firstly, it splits water into hydrogen and oxygen. The oxygen simply passes out of the membrane and then out of the cell, while the hydrogen is essentially set aside. Then, secondly, the remaining energy is used to form adenosine triphosphate (or ATP, the so-called energy currency of the cell) and nicotinamide dinucleotide phosphate (NADPH) (another energy carrier as well as hydrogen carrier for the reactions). Thirdly, ATP and NADPH fuel the next process, through which glucose is formed by the combination of hydrogen and CO_2 (i.e. the dark reactions). A simplified account of these processes can be described by the equation:

$$6CO_2 + 6H_2O + \text{light energy} \rightarrow C_6H_{12}O_6 + 6O_2.$$

Breaking the chemical bonds to complete this process requires 6×10^{-19} joules of energy. A photon of red light has an energy of 3×10^{-19} joules. In other words, the energy absorbed from two photons of red light is sufficient to rearrange bonds between carbon atoms.

All photosynthetic organisms have a thylakoid membrane. The thylakoid membrane freely rests in the cytoplasm of prokaryotes; in eukaryotes, it is contained in chloroplasts. Thylakoids usually contain the green pigment chlorophyll. Different species often have different combinations of photopigments, of which chlorophyll is almost always included. Chlorophyll mainly absorbs red and blue light. Specifically, chlorophyll a absorbs about 70% of the blue light and 50% of the red light that falls on it, while absorbing little blue-green, green, yellow or orange light. An estimated 3% of the solar energy reaching the Earth is captured by marine photoautotrophs; however, only about 33% of the energy absorbed by a chloroplast is ultimately stored in glucose. Numerous accessory pigments compliment chlorophyll by absorbing photons of various wavelengths, maximizing light harvest even where sunlight has been altered by reflection, scattering, etc. Some species are so complete in their ability to capture light that they appear to be almost black.

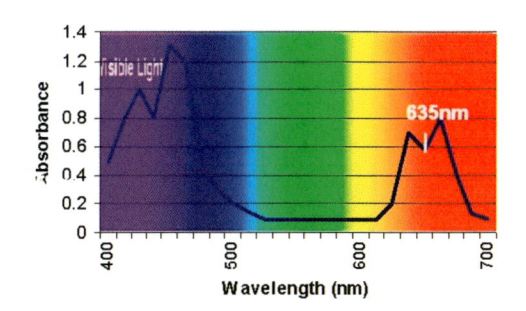

The absorption spectrum of chlorophyll. Zoe Stanyon.

All the same, there is a limit to the amount of light energy a plant can absorb. This limit is reached when light absorption approaches a point of saturation. In this state, productivity plateaus as the cell's photosynthetic machinery is processing photons at the highest possible speed. Even as light intensity surpasses the saturation point, rates of carbon fixation remain unchanged. In a condition termed photoinhibition, productivity can even decrease as the cellular machinery becomes damaged by extremely intense light.

Not all of the fixed carbon ends up as biomass. Much of it is consumed during respiration. Respiration is a process by which the energy stored in glucose is recovered by the plant (or by some organism that eats the plant) for its metabolic energy needs. It is basically the reverse process of photosynthesis:

$$C_6H_{12}O_6 + 6O_2 \rightarrow 6CO_2 + 6H_2O + \text{chemical energy}.$$

Respiration is a sort of slow burn, releasing energy in a controlled manner. Plants respire both day and night. Though much of the energy stored in glucose is used during the day, some of it remains available for use during the nighttime. Since plants both photosynthesize and respire, a certain balance must be maintained. Thus, there is some minimal amount of light energy required to serve a plant's metabolic needs. Due to losses to respiration, not even 1% of the solar energy reaching the Earth is ever transferred to biomass. Compensation intensity is the level of light intensity that must be reached for the gross rate of photosynthesis to equal the gross rate of respiration. Net photosynthesis is either positive when above, or negative when below, the compensation point. Energy released through respiration is stored in ATP until used in reactions throughout the organism. The production of ATP takes place in structures called mitochondria (the so-called powerhouse of the cell). Mitochondria are (like chloroplasts) believed to have originated as an endosymbiotic bacterium.

Plants might be regarded as the most important consumers, since most primary production (50-70%) is consumed during plant respiration. The total energy fixed in photosynthesis is generally referred to as gross primary productivity (GPP). Of this, after accounting for respiration, the total energy that remains is referred to as net primary productivity (NPP), which can be described by the equation:

$$NPP = \Delta B + L + G$$

where ΔB equals the plant biomass produced per unit time, L equals the loss of plant biomass through mortality and G equals loss of plant biomass to herbivory. NPP is usually measured as the mass of carbon fixed per unit area per year (grams C/m^2/year). Nearly half of global primary production is carried out by autotrophic plankton. Temperate phytoplankton fix roughly 50 grams C/m^2/year, but can in many cases reach rates of 120 grams C/m^2/year. The average annual productivity over temperate shelf habitats is 100 grams C/m^2/year (less than 25 grams/C/m^2/year near the shelf's edge and over 300 grams C/m^2/year near exceptionally fertile upwelling zones). Springtime temperate phytoplankton blooms are among the most significant contributors to global productivity. Along the California Current, seasonal upwelling during spring and summer (that is, when light is plentiful) drives productivity to around 125-220 grams/C/m^2/year, roughly 2-4 times the typical productivity of temperate seas.

3. Secondary Production

The generation of new biomass by heterotrophs through the consumption of organic matter is known as secondary production. Secondary productivity is limited principally by the available NPP. The term is sometimes used to refer only to the consumption of primary producers, though it generally refers to all heterotrophic growth. Photoheterotrophs include a somewhat unusual group of microbes that can obtain energy from light, but nevertheless rely on exogenous sources of fixed carbon. The vast majority of consumers are chemoautotrophs, obtaining both their biomass and their energy by eating other organisms. Single-celled herbivores graze on cyanobacteria. Multicellular herbivores such as snails, limpets, chitons and sea urchins graze on macroalgae. These diverse herbivores are preyed on by diverse carnivores. Marine ecologists distinguish several types of predation: (1) herbivory, which involves the consumption of primary producers, (2) carnivory, which involves the consumption of herbivores or other carnivores and (3) parasitism, which involves the consumption, but not death, of one organism (the host) by another plant or animal (the parasite).

Cannibalism is a special type of predation in which both predator and prey are of the same species. The term omnivory is used to describe the consumption of an especially wide variety of food sources. Both omnivory and cannibalism are known to be particularly common in temperate marine food webs. The dead remains of all of these organisms (as well as their waste products) are scavenged and recycled by decomposers.

Where plant life is abundant but herbivory is modest (e.g. salt marshes and seagrass meadows), a considerable amount of energy is diverted through the detrital food chain. Amphipods, fungi and bacteria together shred and ultimately break down dead vegetation. Metazooplankton are important suspension feeders, taking up particulate organic matter (POM) by means of either a sieve or by grabbing it with claw- or jaw-like appendages. Filter-feeding animals transport these nutrients to the seafloor as they convert floating food particles into sinking fecal pellets. Benthic sediment dwellers very much rely on POM as a primary food source (less than 0.5% of the carbon fixed globally each year ever reaches the sea floor). The abundant benthos of the continental shelves rely heavily upon (1) food sources that fall down from the photic zone or (2) are washed out to sea from terrestrial environments. Particularly on deep sea bottoms (where there is no primary production except in areas near cold seeps and hydrothermal vents), these organisms are absolutely dependent upon (1) nutrients carried to them by currents via horizontal transport mechanisms and (2) amalgamated clumps of POM that fall from above (known as marine snow).

Food intake (i.e. gross energy) is not equivalent to secondary production. The energy derived directly from organic material by a consumer is first converted into (1) fecal energy or (2) digestible energy. Any digestible energy is then further converted into (1) urinary energy or (2) metabolizable energy. Metabolizable energy is used for either (1) maintenance and respiration (i.e. resting energy and activity) or (2) growth and reproduction (i.e. productivity). Net secondary productivity (NSP) plus the energy used in respiration equals the energy of assimilation. The ratio of NSP to assimilation is known as secondary production efficiency. Approximately 10% of the carbon uptake of an animal is excreted as waste. And, due to leakage, phytoplankton may lose as much as 40-50% of their internal body fluids to the surrounding waters. These waste products contribute to high levels of solid and dissolved organic matter. While some of this dissolved organic matter (DOM) is lost, various prokaryotes and protists can scavenge these compounds through absorption. Being small (that is, having a large surface-to-volume body ratio) is a distinct advantage in absorbing DOM. Bacteria are very important decomposers, occupying the base of detrital food chains. Many protozooplankton can similarly obtain DOM directly from the water column.

High reproductive rates require large metabolizable energy reserves. Steve Lonhart.

Decomposers and detritivores are integral (though sometimes poorly appreciated) components of the food chain. Decomposition breaks down (or mineralizes) the dead tissues or waste products of other organisms into much simpler substances. Mineralization processes return nutrients to the environment in a form that can again be utilized by autotrophs. Bacterial decomposers take up the DOM and then are eaten by ciliates and flagellates, which release more DOM into the water column, which is again used up by bacteria, and so on. This recovery of energy and its return to the trophic stream is referred to as the microbial loop. Perhaps as much as 60% of the energy in a marine ecosystem passes along this loop.

4. Nutrient Allocation

Of course, it takes more than sugar to build an organism. For this, primary producers require a balanced source of nutrients. The most important of these constituents are certain forms of dissolved inorganic nitrogen and phosphorus, typically occurring at a ratio of 15:1 in seawater. Plants take up nitrogen in the form of ammonium (NH_4^+), nitrite (NO_2^-) and nitrate (NO_3^-) as well as phosphorus in the form of phosphate (PO_4^{3-}). The net chemical reaction for this process can be described by the equation:

$$106\ CO_2 + 122\ H_2O + 16\ HNO_3 + H_3PO_4 = 138\ O_2 + (CH_2O)_{106}(NH_3)_{16}H_3PO_4.$$

In other words, 106 CO_2 molecules, 122 water molecules, 16 nitric acid molecules and one molecule of phosphoric acid react to produce 138 O_2 molecules and some quantity of plant material. So, for every 106 carbon atoms, there are about 16 nitrogen atoms and one phosphorus atom. This basic calculation for the general composition of phytoplankton (a 16:1 ratio of nitrogen to phosphorus) is known as the Redfield ratio. Clearly, nitrogen is consumed in much greater quantities than phosphorus. The most significant aspect of this ratio, however, is that fixed nitrogen is usually the first essential substance to be depleted, making it a limiting nutrient.

Owing to the great store of carbonic acid in the world's oceans, productivity can never be limited by carbon itself. Most productivity is limited by the availability of a few vital nutrients. The most important mineral nutrients in seawater are ammonium, nitrate, phosphate, silicic acid and iron. Ammonium, nitrate, phosphate and silicic acid are all required by primary producers in huge quantities and are therefore referred to as macronutrients, whereas iron, which is required only in small quantities (as little as 0.03 micrograms per liter), is referred to as a micronutrient. Limiting nutrients may be either micronutrients or macronutrients. Most often, producers are limited by the availability of the major macronutrient nitrogen, of which nitrate is the preferred form. Averaging around 0.7 ppm, nitrate is the most concentrated dissolved nitrogenous compound in seawater. The important process through which nitrogen passes from the environment into the food chain and back into the environment is known as the nitrogen cycle. The nitrogen cycle is described as taking place in five steps: (1) nitrogen fixation, (2) assimilation, (3) ammonification, (4) nitrification and (5) denitrification.

All living organisms need a source of fixed nitrogen to survive, grow and reproduce. Though dinitrogen gas (N_2) is quite abundant on Earth (about 80% of the planet's atmosphere is made up of it), only a few organisms can use gaseous nitrogen to synthesize amino acids or genetic material. A vast majority of organisms (including plants) instead need a "fixed" nitrogen source. Nitrogen fixation reactions break the strong bonds between nitrogen atoms, converting dinitrogen into ammonia or nitrate. Some gaseous nitrogen is fixed through purely physical processes (e.g. lightning, forest fires); most nitrogen fixation is carried out biologically, usually using the enzyme nitrogenase. The equivalent energy of 12 grams of glucose is required to fix a single gram of nitrogen. The small handful of organisms that are capable of fixing nitrogen are known as diazotrophs. Though the group includes many unrelated species, all diazotrophs are prokaryotes. Though some are heterotrophic, most are autotrophs. Cyanobacteria are the major autotrophic nitrogen fixers in marine ecosystems.

As fixed nitrogen flows through the food chain, it is either assimilated into the biomass of some organism or it is excreted as a nitrogenous waste product (usually ammonia). Ammonia is subsequently converted to nitrate through a process known as bacterial nitrification. The nitrifying bacteria are a group of aerobic chemoautotrophs that together convert ammonium to nitrate. This group is composed of the nitrite and nitrate bacteria. Nitrite bacteria obtain energy by converting ammonia to nitrite; nitrate bacteria obtain energy by converting nitrite to nitrate. Denitrifying bacteria reduce nitrate back into N_2, completing the cycle. Denitrifiers inhabit oxygen-poor habitats such as deep sediments and stagnant inshore environments. Because denitrification somewhat outpaces nitrogen fixation globally, nitrogen limitation is the norm in many regions.

Nutrient concentrations are generally lowest in the surface waters. As organisms grow, die and sink, their carcasses transport nutrients from the euphotic zone to the deep, which can only be returned en masse through the action of upwelling. The biologically driven transfer of nitrogen between the atmosphere and the ocean depths is known as the biological pump. The amount of new biomass that draws from a local nutrient source (such as the excretions of zooplankton) is referred to as regeneration production; the amount of new biomass that draws from deep-water nutrient sources is referred to as new production.

5. Distribution and Zonation

Categorized by proximity to the coastline, all marinelife may be divided into four major groups: (1) pelagic species, which occur in open waters and do not approach land, continental shelves or any sea bed, (2) offshore species, which rarely approach land but are not truly pelagic and occur at water depths of 50-200 meters (165-655 feet), (3) inshore species, which occur near the coastline at water depths of less than 50 meters and (4) littoral species, which occur along the coastal fringe between the high- and low-tide marks.

Every species is distributed across some particular geographic area (or range). The area used by an individual organism is referred to as its home range. Few species are distributed evenly across their range; rather, they tend to be concentrated in areas that present minimal environmental stress. However, this leads to crowding and resource depletion, presenting its own challenges. The particular set of stressors encountered in a given habitat changes directionally with gradients of both water depth and distance from the shore.

All organisms experience stressors that can injure or kill them or inhibit their ability to reproduce. Stress can be characterized as being either biotic or abiotic. Particularly in coastal waters, stressors tend to be mainly abiotic in the shallows and mainly biotic at greater depths. The most important causes of biotic stress include (1) competition and (2) herbivory/predation. The most important causes of abiotic stress include (1) desiccation, (2) currents/wave action, (3) low or high salinity, (4) extreme temperature, (5) oxygen deprivation and, in the case of photoautotrophs, (6) light deprivation. Together, they are responsible for the lateral zonation of species.

The effects of desiccation and submergence are most intense around the supralittoral zone. Patterns of immersion/emersion are determined by the tidal range and slope of the shore. During low-tide in some flats, several square miles of seabottom might be exposed; conversely, where there are steep shores or cliffs, only narrow strips of seabottom will ever be exposed. Adaptations that counter the effects of desiccation include closing up, exuding a protective slime coat and retreating to wetter locations (tidepools, weed wrack, etc.). Some algae of the high shore can recover from water losses as severe as 60-90%. Many intertidal macroalgae and sea anemones avoid drying by secreting copious amounts of mucus. Infauna burrow deeply into the ever-moist soft substrate. Small, flighty animals of all kinds (the shore crab (*Carcinus maenus*), the glass shrimp (*Palaemon elegans*), the sand eel (*Ammodytes lanceolatus*), the butterfly blenny (*Blennius ocellaris*), etc.) follow the movement of the tides, chasing the shallows just below the shoreline. Oysters (e.g. *Crassostrea* spp.) and other intertidal bivalves simply seal themselves up tightly within their shells. Organisms that cannot tolerate prolonged immersion (e.g. salt marsh grasses) can colonize only the uppermost parts of the shore. The major North American salt marsh cord grass species *Spartina alternaflora* is capable of growing only along the

Though it occurs in an equatorial region, *Bodianus bimaculatus* inhabits steep outer reef slopes and thus is likely adapted to tolerate chilly conditions. Felicia McCaulley.

high-tide line; rushes (*Juncus* spp.) and other grasses grow just above it. In Northern Europe, *Spartina townsendii* can run straight into shallowly submerged beds of algae (*Enteromorpha* spp.) or seagrass (*Zostera nana*). Similarly across the temperate Northern American coast, widgeongrass (*Ruppia maritima*) can be found growing right up to the edge of eelgrass (*Zostera* spp.) meadows.

The effects of wave impact and tidal currents are most intense over hard bottoms, where organisms cannot burrow into the substrate to hide. To withstand the powerful surges in these environments, organisms must be capable of attaching strongly to the rocky surface. Small barnacles cement themselves firmly to rock just within reach of the crashing waves. Mussels (e.g. *Mytilus* spp.) secrete strong fibers with which they anchor themselves firmly to the rock. Macroalgae are similarly anchored to rock by means of a flexible stipe that is attached to a sturdy, tendril-like structure called a holdfast. Some creatures such as sea urchins (e.g. *Strongylocentrotus* spp.) and boring clams (e.g. Family Pholadidae) may slowly carve out a depression into the solid stone for additional protection.

The effects of salinity stress are strongest in surface waters and estuaries. Particularly where mixing is minimal, strong gradients of salinity can develop in surface waters following periods of heavy rainfall or evaporation. Average seawater salinities vary somewhat between latitudes due to differences in weather pattern; while dissolves salts make up about 3.5% of the mass of seawater on average, it is often as low as 3.3% in temperate regions and as high as 3.7% in the tropics. The highest surface water salinities in the ocean are found in the region from 20° to 30° N and S, where precipitation rates are the lowest and evaporation rates are the highest. At depths greater than 1,000 meters (3,280 feet), salinity is far more uniform (typically 34.5-35.0 ppt). Salinity can reach extremes in semi-confined bodies. For example, because the Baltic Sea is cold and so does not readily evaporate, and is fed by many large rivers, its waters can range as low in salinity as 10 ppt. On the other hand, in the Mediterranean Sea, where evaporation rates are high and there is relatively little river water influx, salinity can range as high as 40 ppt. In estuarine environments, salinity gradients are strongest near the estuary head. These sharp gradients result in a highly localized species distribution.

Inshore fish species (such as *Parablennius laticlavius*) are slightly more tolerant of fluctuating salinity. Ian Skipworth.

Benthic estuarine organisms can be categorized according to their salt tolerance: (1) stenohaline species that can penetrate estuary waters to 30 ppt salinity, such as the common cockle (*Cerastoderma edule*), (2) euryhaline marine species that can penetrate up to 30 ppt salinity, such as the amphipod *Corophium volutator*, (3) true brackish species such as horned wrack (*Fucus ceranoides*) and (4) true freshwater species such as some insects (many during their larval stages) and the isopod *Asellus aquaticus*. It is not altogether uncommon for neritic fish species to undergo some part of their life cycle in fresh waters. Those that spawn in freshwater but grow out in the ocean (e.g American shad (*Alosa sapidissima*)) are referred to as anadromous, while those that spawn at sea but grow out in freshwater (such as the American eel (*Anguilla rostrata*)) are referred to as catadromous.

Most populations of the three-spined stickleback (*Gasterosteus aculeatus*) are anadromous. Barrett Paul.

The effects of thermal stress are most intense in the intertidal zone, where rapidly changing air temperatures can shock an emersed organism. Proteins denature at temperatures above 45°C (112°F); cells rupture as they freeze. Ectotherms are organisms that cannot control their own body temperature, which fluctuates along with the ambient temperature. There are relatively few marine endothermic (or warm-blooded) species (i.e. seabirds and marine mammals) with a great many species (e.g. fish and invertebrates) being ectothermic (or cold-blooded). Ectothermic organisms can function metabolically only within a narrow environmental temperature range. There is some ideal body temperature for each species; in this respect, the term coldwater itself may be somewhat relative (some arctic fish species are unable to tolerate waters as "warm" as 10°C (50°F)). In most ectotherms, every increase of 10 degrees C (18 degrees F) results in a doubling or tripling of oxygen consumption. Generally, the metabolic rate is halved with each 10 degree C (18 degree F) decrease of temperature below the much narrower optimal range. For instance, if some cold-blooded animal that is acclimated to a water temperature of 25°C (77°F) is suddenly chilled to 5°C (41°F), its metabolism will drop to a quarter of the initial rate—a 50% drop for the first 10°C and another 50% drop for the second. Rapid, extreme shifts in body temperature such as this are typically fatal.

Because ectotherms cannot regulate their body temperatures physiologically, they must rely on certain physical and behavioral adaptations to avoid overheating or freezing. Some invertebrates prevent overheating through evaporative cooling. Some prevent freezing by taking on a dark coloration, which absorbs more solar energy. Fish generally abscond to deeper, more thermally stable waters during low-tide. However, during the coldest winter months, polar and cold-temperate fish must either (1) migrate to a warmer region or (2) possess some means of resistance to freezing. Many arctic, Antarctic and North Temperate species rely on the latter strategy. These fishes survive in chilled waters by either (1) elevating their base metabolic rates and remaining active or (2) entering a state of dormancy (or semihibernation) to conserve energy for the duration of the cold season. Nonmigratory species must depress the freezing point of their body fluids to just below that of seawater by producing various antifreeze compounds. Sodium chloride is the predominant antifreeze of marine fishes, with other substances such as calcium, potassium, glucose and urea accounting for something like another tenth of a degree C (0.18 degrees F) of depression. Nevertheless, many Antarctic and some cold-temperate fishes achieve a doubling of freezing point depression by combining high sodium chloride concentrations with antifreeze proteins. These compounds usually consist of linked amino acids (as in peptides), oftentimes with carbohydrate branches (as in glycopeptides). They appear to work by attaching to forming ice crystals, interfering with further ice formation. The blood antifreeze levels of many North Temperate fish species (e.g. tomcod, winter flounder and short-horned sculpin) fluctuate with seasonal changes; in response to a reduction of temperature and photoperiod, the liver increases synthesis of antifreeze proteins.

Oxygen is not very soluble in seawater. Its solubility is affected by salinity and water temperature, decreasing sharply with increasing salinity and temperature. Wind-driven mixing increases the exchange of gasses between the surface ocean waters and the atmosphere. Chilly thermohaline currents deliver oxygen to the deepest seas. Actually, oxygen concentrations are usually lowest in the mid-depths (100-1,000 meters (300-3,200 feet)), where there is little exchange with surface waters or deep currents. The effects of oxygen deprivation (or hypoxia) are most intense in environments where net rates of respiration exceed net rates of primary production. Such may occur in dead zones, which are bottom waters that are anoxic due to an overload of sinking organic matter.

The effects of light deprivation on marine plants intensify with increasing depth. For example, a depth-dependent zonation of phytoplankton species (with different species concentrated at different depths) develops in response to light attenuation from the surface to the compensation depth. Depth-dependent zonation can result from the aggressive vertical growth of certain kelp species. The giant kelp (*Macrocystis pyrifera*) creates a massive, shady surface canopy. Beneath this canopy at around two meters (six feet) over the seafloor is a second canopy created by mid-sized kelps (mainly *Laminaria* and *Pterygophora*). Beneath these kelps is a third layer of shorter, leafy red and brown algae as well as crusts of red coralline algae. Red algae dominate in the shadowy bottom waters; a turf of filamentous red algae and encrusting red coralline algae cover the surface of the substrate between macroalgal holdfasts. Because light availability is crucial to the survival of marine plants (which provide a primary source of food and habitat structure), the most biologically rich of benthic habitats are usually situated at depths of less than 55-60 meters (180-195 feet).

6. Community Structure

A biological community consists of a group of species that inhabit a given area and engage in some sort of interaction. The terms community and assemblage are sometimes used synonymously, though in stricter terms community is meant to refer to all of the organisms in an ecosystem while assemblage refers specifically to a group of taxonomically or behaviorally related species. One of the most basic units of a biological community, after that of the individual, is a population. A population simply is a group of related individuals (generally of the same species) that inhabit the same area at the same time. Where resources are unlimited, populations grow exponentially (at the maximal rate of growth, r). However, because resources are almost always finite, there is a maximal population size (or carrying capacity, K) that the environment can support at a given time. Growth and reproduction is not unlimited. Growth rates and carrying capacities are determined by a number of environmental conditions. A limiting factor is any biotic (e.g. shading by another plant) or abiotic (e.g. light attenuation) factor that limits the growth of a population. This limitation of resources leads to competition.

Competition may exist between members of the same species (i.e. intraspecific) or between members of two different species (i.e. interspecific). Competitive interactions can be characterized as either scramble or contest competition. Organisms compete directly for some limiting resource in a scramble, acquiring as much of it as they can, whereas in contest competition they directly injure each other through physical force (plants and invertebrates tend to use the former strategy, while fish and other vertebrates tend to use the latter). Schoener (1985) describes six categories of competition: (1) consumptive (or exploitive) competition, which involves claiming resources, (2) preemptive competition, which involves quickly acquiring space, (3) overgrowth competition, which involves growing over and ultimately smothering a competitor, (4) chemical competition, which involves the use of noxious or toxic compounds, (5) territorial competition, which involves direct attacks for space and (6) encounter competition, which involves direct but fleeting interactions that take place during contests for a specific resource. Exploitive competition is the most common of these groups in marine environments.

The terms r-selection and K-selection are used to describe the selection of traits that determine fecundity and survivorship, favoring rapid population growth at low density r and favoring competitive superiority at densities near carrying capacity K_r. Generally, r-selected species (e.g.

Temperate coastal ecosystems support large populations of big, carnivorous fishes (such as this *Sebastes miniatus*). Chad King.

Fishes that guard eggs and nests (such as this *Parma kermadecensis*) tend toward a K-selected reproductive strategy. Ian Skipworth.

This *Gibbonsia* sp. kelpfish is well camouflaged amongst the coralline algae. Chad King.

Every bit of space can be precious on a temperate reef. Chad King.

The mado *Atypichthys latus* occupies headlands and offshore islands. Ian Skipworth.

broadcast spawners) have high growth rates, invade less-crowded spaces and produce numerous offspring (with each having a relatively low probability of surviving to adulthood); *K*-selected species (e.g. nest tenders) have lower growth rates, invade the most favorable spaces and produce fewer offspring (with each having a relatively high probability of surviving to adulthood).

Intense competition can lead to competitive exclusion, whereby an inferior competitor is completely extirpated from an area by some superior competitor. The effects of competitive exclusion can be quite localized in highly variable environments. One notable feature of littoral hard-bottom habitats is how the distribution of its predominant inhabitants changes dramatically over short distances. This tendency is most famously described by Joseph Connell (1961). Connell sought to understand why the brown barnacle *Chthamalus* and the white barnacle *Balanus* were concentrated in different bands along the rocky shore, with the former always appearing above the latter, as the larvae of both species occur together. *Balanus* could not settle in spots where he removed *Chthamalus*, suggesting that *Balanus* is incapable of surviving desiccation in the upper intertidal. Though *Chthamalus* could settle in spots where he removed *Balanus*, the latter always outcompeted (through crushing, lifting and smothering) and eventually eliminated the former. Interestingly, the severity of the exclusion of *Chthamalus* by *Balanus* was found to be lessened somewhat through predation by the snail *Thais*, which distinctly prefers *Balanus* and has a reach just into the lower range of the barnacle zone. From this study he demonstrated how the lower distribution of littoral organisms depends mainly upon biotic factors (e.g. competition and predation) while the upper distribution depends mainly upon abiotic factors (e.g. desiccation, heat stress).

The two major factors that promote lateral zonation are (1) competition for space and (2) competition for light or food. Coastal environments generally become more hospitable with increasing distance from the shore. There are often just a few, huge populations of species on the high shore, whereas the lower parts are inhabited by smaller populations of numerous species. Those species that can tolerate a wide range of physical conditions are termed eurytopic, while those with narrow ranges of tolerance are termed stenotopic. Within every species' tolerance range is an optimal range, where rates of growth and reproduction are highest. A given habitat might be optimal for multiple, competing species. Thus, in order to claim space there, a species must be a superior competitor. For that reason, inferior competitors must be superior invaders, able to colonize less crowded (though suboptimal) spaces where conditions are just within their tolerance range. For example, on the rocky shores of the British Isles, varying tolerances and competitive abilities result in the strong segregation of four kelp species; from the top of the shore to the bottom, one might encounter channel wrack (*Pelvetia canaliculata*), then spiral wrack (*Fucus spiralis*), then bladder wrack (*F. vesiculosus*) and then saw wrack (*F. serratus*).

Those species that have the greatest biomass in a given area are referred to as dominant species. Entire communities may depend upon a dominant species. For example, the lugworm *Arenicola marina* of Northwest European sandy shores, which is capable of reaching population densities as high as 70 individuals per square meter, provides a vital food source for numerous other species. However, dominant species (which are often superior competitors) can completely smother out all other species from a community. This kind of total competitive exclusion may be prevented by the presence of organisms that prey on the dominants. A classic example of this phenomenon is provided by Thomas Paine (1969). Paine removed the starfish *Pisaster* from beds of the mussel *Mytilus*, upon which it preferentially feeds. He noted that *Mytilus*, a superior competitor for space, expanded rapidly at the expense of other organisms ranging from seaweeds to anemones to chitons. In other words, starfish predation actually increased biodiversity in the area. What was most significant is the disproportionately large influence that a *Pisaster* population has on its community despite its relatively low biomass. Paine went on to introduce the term keystone species for this and any organism that performs a critical ecological function.

The influence of herbivory on community structure is especially strong in temperate ecosystems. The Pacific sea otter (*Enhydra lutris*) is considered to be a keystone species in East Pacific kelp forests where it feeds on sea urchins. Sea urchins such as *Strongylocentrotus* are voracious algal grazers

The toado *Canthigaster callisterna* feeds heavily on small benthic invertebrates. Ian Skipworth.

Rockfishes (such as this *Sebastes caurinus*) are slow-growing but long-lived. Chad King.

The triplefin *Notoclinops segmentatus* is known to remove parasites from larger fishes. Ian Skipworth.

Predation can be intense on the rocky reef. Chad King.

and can, if not controlled by otters, quickly eradicate an entire bed of kelp. Where sea otters are plentiful, kelp communities may become very complex, developing a surface layer of *Alaria fistulosa*, a secondary canopy of four species of *Laminaria* and a prostrate (noncanopy) layer of *Agarum clathratum*. A remarkably similar effect can be observed in the Mediterranean Ocean, where the overfishing of urchin predators (e.g. the spider crab (*Maja crispata*) and fishes such as *Coris julis* and *Labrus merula*) has led to the overpopulation of the dominant sea urchin herbivore *Paracentrotus lividus* and subsequent losses of *Laminaria* and *Cystoseira* forest.

Competition for vital resources can be reduced through a kind of sharing made possible through niche partitioning. A niche is simply the role that an organism plays in an ecosystem. Niche partitioning occurs when competing organisms exploit the shared resource in different ways. In the case of temporal partitioning, competitors use a shared resource at different times. For example, two fish may be able to singly occupy the same resting space if one (a nocturnal species) uses it during the day and the other (a diurnal species) uses it at night.

Pioneer species are those organisms that are the early colonizers of barren, freshly disturbed habitat. Some pioneers can actually create habitat. The invertebrate animals that generate biogenic structures in the temperate regions are not stony corals, but rather are certain oysters, polychaete worms and vermetid gastropods. For example, sedimentary polychaete worm shoals (such as those formed by *Petaloproctus socialis* and *Sabellaria* spp.) and the intertwined tubes of vermetid gastropods increase habitat complexity in benthic environments. Some oysters (e.g. *Crassostrea* spp.) play the role of pioneer species in some silty estuaries, where they provide the requisite hard substratum upon which many other sessile invertebrates as well as macroalgae can attach. The oysters themselves recruit to the shells of other oysters, eventually constructing

Hard surfaces that have been denuded by urchin grazing are quickly colonized by sessile invertebrates such as *Corynactis*. Claire Fackler.

reefs that can rise several meters above the sea bed. As many as 300 marine invertebrate species may be found in some Northwest Atlantic oyster shell habitats. Oyster bed communities of the Chesapeake Bay include other mollusks such as mussels, giant whelk (*Buscyon cavica*) and soft shelled clam (*Mya arenaria*), crustaceans such as barnacles, amphipods and crabs, various seaweeds, sea stars (*Asterina* spp.) and the notoriously ugly oyster toadfish (*Opsanus tau*).

A thick turf of articulated coralline algae and the presence of zooxanthellate sea anemones (*Anemonia* sp.) suggests a rather brightly sunlit environment. Que2.

Well-crafted aquarium systems will look presentable as well as function efficiently. Michiel Vos.

Stark environments are altered by the activity of pioneers, and are then colonized by other species which in turn further reshape the environs. Food chains are short in recently established communities, getting longer as the community matures. In time, a different and usually more diverse climax habitat emerges as the community structure reaches an equilibrium. This multi-staged process is known as ecological succession. A situation in which a species colonizes a previously uninhabited area (e.g. a recently disturbed site) is called primary succession. An example of this may be the colonization by *Postelsia palmaeformis* of bare rock scoured by logs during recent storms. Secondary succession occurs with transitory changes of species composition and habitat usage. An example of this may be the return of giant kelps after denudation by urchins. Various successional stages can occur simultaneously in patchy habitats that are subjected to intense, highly localized disturbance events. For example, in New Zealand fjords, frequent landslides exert a continuous influence over intertidal communities. By disrupting habitat structure across ecosystems, ecological disturbance can actually promote biodiversity; then again, it can wipe out an entire species. Really, our present biosphere can be thought of as the product of all past and present cycles of disturbance and ecological succession.

IV. Aquarium Systems
1. Conceptualization and Planning

Whether you intend to maintain a marine aquarium system of any kind for work, for pleasure, or for both, your activities will serve some purpose. The best way to insure that this purpose is duly served (within a budget) is to (1) develop a conceptualized design of the completed, running system and (2) formulate a complete, detailed plan to carry out its construction and ongoing operation. Both the concept and the plan should be fully developed *before* making any equipment or livestock purchases. Of course, the conceptualization phase of any project takes place during the initial design activities; here, the scope of project is declared and lists of essential pieces of equipment and system design features are made.

Whether it is to be your first aquarium or your tenth, it is best to ask yourself why you want the particular system that you want; ask what you want it to do. Determine as specifically as possible what you expect to accomplish with the installation. For example, if you wish to operate commercially as an *Ulva* farm, do not just state "to make money" as a goal; declare something more explicit like "to produce 1,500 kilograms of dried product per day at five days per week indoors using a recirculating aquarium grow-bed system, fish emulsion-based fertilizers and all-artificial lighting." Even if you wish simply to keep an aquarium for private amusement, you should clarify your goals. Settle on something like "to develop a stable, mature *Posidonia* meadow community (55 gallons) with a focus on bay pipefish (*Syngnathus leptorhyncus*) and northern seahorses (*Hippocampus erectus*) that is calming to watch."

Establish a long list of desired aquarium species. You should place your most desired species at the top of this list, and then cut from that list any species that are incompatible (either biotically or abiotically) with the top species. Using all available resources, thoroughly research both the natural history and the captive care of any prospective livestock. Your exhaustive research will help you to (1) determine the needs of the desired species and (2) determine which techniques/technologies you will employ to best fulfill those needs. From this you can conceive of the shape, size and type of system to construct. Make numerous drawings (or better yet, if you know how to make them, CAD illustrations) of the aquarium, the cabinetry and all associated equipment. Then, perhaps most importantly, imagine every possible thing that could go wrong with the system. Incorporate any solutions to potential problems into the final conceptual design.

The planning phase can begin only when the aquarium system has been fully conceptualized and complete lists of all needed items are made. Good planning starts with the provision of some kind of budget. Most often, expenses are categorized and assigned either to a one-time installation (i.e. start-up) budget or to a monthly or annual maintenance budget. Aquarium systems are expensive; good aquarium systems are even more expensive. It is therefore best to be realistic from the onset while projecting both initial and ongoing spending for the project. There certainly will be some minimal system size for your particular needs, and you will indeed want to avoid committing yourself to early failure by building an undersized system. Still, it does not make sense to purchase more tank than you can afford to properly maintain. Bear in mind that monthly operating costs, as well as set-up cost, will increase with any increase in system size. We all want our things to be bigger and better. That notwithstanding, few of us can afford to have both. Even though we are relying principally upon our imagination during the conceptualization phase, there is no use for wishful thinking. A system that "might work" is a system that will inevitably fail. Choose a sensibly designed system that gives precedence to performance. Considerations such as convenience, aesthetics, novelty or pricing should carry little weight here. Failure is always more expensive than success; a healthy and functional 15-gallon aquarium is surely preferable to an unhealthy, malfunctioning 150-gallon system.

If you are starting to feel overwhelmed by sticker shock, you may have begun to appreciate the kind of financial commitment that a properly equipped coldwater marine aquarium (of any size) can be. Keeping to a budget is an inherently long-term commitment. In the long run, value is always better than price. Cheap carbon, for example, has little value if its active life is short and its performance is suboptimal. Once you calculate (based upon the needs of the desired species) the price of the smallest, complete system that is appropriate for the livestock, estimate the average monthly cost of system maintenance. Allow for unexpected or infrequent expenses such as light bulb replacement. This may be the time to make some hard choices. If you do not have the resources to meet either your set-up or your monthly budget, you simply cannot cut major components of the system (e.g. forego a protein skimmer) to make up the difference. That is, you cannot skimp on the system. You must either cut the stocking list, reduce the scale of the entire build or simply postpone the project until the required funds become available. So, if the only reason for including a state-of-the-art, high-output lighting system in a design is to keep just a few zooxanthellate sea anemones or pieces of kelp, and those anemones or algae are not to be key features of the aquarium community, it may not be too shrewd to cut these organisms (and hence high-end light fixtures) from the concept.

The purpose of the planning phase is to help you to meet your objectives—make things happen—in a controlled and informed manner. Carried out in the best possible spirit, planning is less about obsessive price shopping and more about establishing good relationships with competent equipment and livestock suppliers. Moreover, planning does not merely involve the apportionment of funds and the acquisition of goods, but also the setting of meaningful benchmarks. Though all short- and long-term plans should be completely drafted before the first piece of hose is purchased, planning certainly does not end when the tank is filled and the system is plugged in. Actually, the planning phase may never really end; your thoughtfully constructed microcosm may, as a living community, always be a work in process. In the very least you should create a stocking plan, wherein the introduction of certain species coincides with particular stages in the biological succession of the captive ecosystem. It may take months or even years until the final, mature climax community has emerged. It is certainly acceptable to change plans along the way. But, one way or another, coldwater aquaria must be constructed and managed in a well-organized manner for effective long-term operation.

2. Tanks and Cabinetry

The most difficult parts of a complete, running aquarium system to replace are the tank and cabinetry. Thus, if there is one thing you must get right on the first shot, this is it. The four main considerations to make while selecting a tank are (1) size, (2) shape, (3) composition and (4) thickness. The minimum size of the tank will be dictated by the needs of the desired species, whereas its maximum size will be dictated by the needs (if not budget) of the aquarist. Obviously, the system must physically fit (with all necessary working space) into the proposed installation site. The shape of the tank will be determined by the main type of aquascape and organisms to be kept. You might opt for a tall shape if your aim is to showcase kelps; you might choose a flattened shape if your system will be dominated by burrowing fish and invertebrates. Be aware that a tall tank (which will require thicker panels to support greater water pressure) can be more costly than a long tank of

This large fiberglass tub is densely stocked with juvenile flounder in an aquacultural setting. Note the mesh/PVC lids. Kenneth Wingerter.

This custom chiller box (with sound-proofing panels and synchronized box fan) positions the unit so that all air must pass through it; the lid has been removed here for viewing. Jon Olav Bjørndal.

equal volume. Be especially wary of unusual tank shapes (globes, cones, vases, etc.), as they oftentimes are difficult to service and can make providing adequate water circulation a lot more complicated.

There are several choices of aquarium construction. Swimming pools, storage bins and feed troughs that are constructed of various plastic or reinforced fiberglass materials are common in aquacultural applications. Specially constructed round or rectangular tanks (sometimes fitted with windows for lateral viewing) are gaining popularity. Many such culture vessels incorporate a depression on the tank bottom with a valve, facilitating the collection and removal of settled solid waste. Pond lining might be used over a foundation of cinder block, wood frame, etc. in certain applications (e.g. touch pools). Sometimes materials such as treated wood panels (e.g. marine grade plywood) are used for the bottoms and sides of tanks. Generally, viewing panels are set over round or rectangular cutouts (water-side) with silicone; glazing may be acrylic or glass. Being as they provide excellent (that is, energy-saving) thermal insulation, wood panel tanks are most often favored by keepers of larger coldwater aquaria. While the wood panels themselves are quite sturdy, these tanks must be properly braced (using the right type of fastener and glue for the particular grade of wood) to ensure structural integrity. The wood should also be completely protected from moisture. This will require multiple coats of a durable, nontoxic, waterproof epoxy paint, perhaps with a protective painted fiberglass or laminated plastic outer lining.

The most accessible and affordable style (particularly for smaller, more conventional aquaria) is still glass. One common complaint about the use of glass tanks for coldwater systems (especially in warm, humid areas), however, is the condensation of water on the tank panes (or sweating). Because the dew point is just around 13°C (55°F) where there is an air temperature of 24°C (75°F) and a relative humidity of 50%, poorly insulated coldwater glass enclosures may sweat profusely. The resulting moisture will not only obscure viewing, but can, as it drips from the tank, also damage equipment and cabinetry. Some types of window laminate (e.g. 3M™ Ultra Series) have been used successfully to inhibit sweating on glass tanks. Some glass-constructed tanks that are specially made for coldwater applications have a double pane construction (and insulating air space) that averts sweating. Still, while double pane glass is arguably the best option in terms of insulation, these tanks are inordinately bulky and cumbersome.

A particularly effectual material for most conventional coldwater aquarium applications is acrylic plastic. It is true that acrylic materials are scratched more easily than glass; it is also true that scratches are more easily repaired on acrylic than on glass. Acrylic materials are easier to work with (cut, drill, etc.) than glass. Moreover, acrylic tanks are far lighter, a bit clearer and way more leak-proof than glass tanks. They do require substantial bracing at the top, which can be somewhat restrictive when cleaning or aquascaping. Most important to coldwater marine aquarists, however, are the superior insulative properties of acrylic materials. For this reason, tank panels composed of acrylic need not be quite as thick as those composed of glass. In order to provide adequate support, acrylic panels of a minimal thickness of 3/8 inch, 1/2 inch and 3/4 inch are generally used for tank heights above 18 inches, 24 inches and 30 inches respectively. Under normal conditions, a thickness of at least 1/2 inch will prevent most sweating; for very tall tanks or where the possibility of sweating must be completely eliminated, a thickness of at least 1 inch is recommended. Considering that glass panels must be around twice as thick to achieve similar results, single panel glass tanks are usually deemed to be less practical than acrylic for most coldwater enclosures.

There is little margin for error when constructing even a modestly sized tank. If you do not possess all of the proper tools and skills for this job, it is advisable to turn the task over to a professional aquarium fabricator or purchase a factory assembled product. The same can be said of the tank stand, which must faithfully bear a considerable amount of weight. Aquarium stands are best constructed from strong materials such as solid, treated hardwoods or coated metals (stainless steel, extruded aluminum, etc.) rather than cheap but flimsy materials such as pressboard. Unless they are properly pretreated, concrete blocks can crumble when exposed to moisture and therefore can make a dangerously poor choice of aquarium stand. An especially desirable feature in an aquarium stand is an open, level, unobstructed interior accessed through a large front opening with a wide-swinging door. This makes it much easier to install, hide, access and remove equipment. Avoid stands that have a brace running through the middle of (that is, blocking) the front opening. Regardless of the size of any opening at the back of the stand (particularly if it is pushed up against a wall), the front opening should be large enough to remove all components contained within, including the sump. Otherwise, it may become

Josh Groves approves of this specialty coldwater acrylic aquarium with locking (that is, octopus proof) lid. Kenneth Wingerter.

Particularly when designing public exhibits, easy access to the tank and its inhabitants is a key consideration. Kenneth Wingerter.

necessary at some point to shut down, empty and move the entire system just to perform some minor repair on a plumbing line, add a piece of equipment, or whatever.

Placement of the aquarium will not only have an effect on how you will view it but also affect how well it can operate. For obvious reasons, it is best to keep coldwater aquaria away from direct sunlight, fireplaces, vent ducts and other heat sources. Situating the stand even just a little bit away from (rather than against) the wall will allow for more ventilation, reduce the amount of moisture and salt creep on the wall and facilitate cleaning or retrieving small items that may fall there. Chose an area that is safe from unhappy incidents with doors, pets, etc. Most importantly, be sure not only that the stand can support the filled tank, but that the flooring can support the entire aquarium system. For the most support, the stand is best situated parallel to the floor joists. Being as 4.5 liters (one gallon) of saltwater weighs about 4.5 kg (10 lbs.), a 1,000-liter (220-gallon) aquarium will weigh at least a ton. If you plan on installing a system larger than 680 liters (180 gallons), or if you are unsure of the structural strength of your floor, contact a professional to better assess the site. Thankfully, aquarium/flooring collapses are not common, but can nevertheless cause very serious damage and injury when they occur.

The top of an aquarium stand may be an open frame or a solid platform. Holes often must be carefully measured out and drilled into stand platforms to accommodate plumbing (e.g. overflow lines) before placement of the tank. Some aquarists place a thin sheet of rubber or polystyrene between the tank and stand to correct a slightly imperfect level as well as equalize pressure against the bottom panel. When the tank has been placed on the stand in its permanent position, recheck the level on all sides. If the stand does not have adjustable feet, use shims to make any necessary adjustments. Continue to check the level as you fill the tank.

The tank should be securely covered with a lid. Tight-fitting lids help to reduce evaporative water loss and salt spray, keep light fixtures dry and prevent items from falling into the aquarium. They are also pretty good at keeping aquarium livestock in the tank and children and pets out of the tank. Lids with special locking mechanisms are available for those keeping especially determined and capable escape artists (e.g. octopuses). Some aquarists additionally cover the aquarium with a canopy. A tank canopy can effectively conceal and protect light fixtures, but should also have a small fan to forcefully remove the heat that they produce. Canopies usually are painted or stained to match the stand. In cases where the aquarium cabinetry will be exposed to direct sunlight, light-colored finishes will help to reduce heat absorption. A chiller may be concealed in a special sound-dampening cabinet of its own. This can be of a material, style and finish that matches the rest of the cabinetry. Chiller boxes are fitted with vents and fans that allow for the free movement of air through the unit.

Even if the cabinetry is made from water-resistant materials (and it certainly ought to be), it is good practice to take every possible measure to protect it from moisture. The use of small mounted fans can help to control humidity and condensation within the aquarium stand. A stand should be replaced immediately upon the discovery of any sign of water damage (swelling, rot, rust, etc.).

3. Sumps and Refugia

A sump is really just some vessel that serves as a central reservoir for the entire aquarium system. Sumps are most commonly placed below the main tank, usually hidden within the aquarium cabinetry. However, in some cases, it may be removed to some remote area (usually the lower level of a building such as a basement or cellar). It can be made from any water-tight tank or tub. Large, heavy-duty plastic beverage coolers can be modified to make excellent sumps for coldwater systems. There are, however, a number of attributes that can make any sump much more effective and serviceable.

So long as you have the space for it, a bigger sump is a better sump. In some cases, the sump may contain a greater volume of water than the display tank. A larger sump will not only increase your overall system water volume but will also provide enough space to concentrate equipment such as pumps, probes and filter components in a single, highly accessible area. It may be divided into sections by baffles. The vertical position of each baffle can be arranged to direct flow through either the top or the bottom waters of the sump. It may also have specialized compartments to hold particular filter components. It should have a tight lid to reduce evaporation and spray. It can, like the main tank, rest upon a thin cushion of rubber or Styrofoam. If not of a thick acrylic (or similarly insulated) construction, the walls of the sump should be lined with sheets of water-proof thermal insulation material.

The sump must be tall enough to accommodate the last bit of overflowing water that will spill down when the main pump is cut. It is a good idea to place markings on the sump as a visual reference for water level—a low mark to set the minimal operating level and a high mark to set the point to which the water level in the sump will rise when the main pump is off. Be careful to not allow evaporation to drop the level below a pump intake; do not maintain a water level in the sump that is so high that it overflows when the pump stalls.

Refugia have captured the imaginations of inventive aquarists since their introduction by Dr. Walter Adey at the Smithsonian Institution in the early 1980s. A refugium is either a sump or a compartment within a sump that is used to retain plants or animals. Refugia are mostly physically separated from, but share water with, the main tank. An early use of refugia was as an incubator for small crustaceans (especially amphipods) and fast-growing macroalgae. However, they may house anything from seagrasses to sponges to tube anemones. They may be heavily stocked with certain bivalves for the purpose of clearing excessive phytoplankton blooms. They may in some cases be a great place for a small, injured animal to recuperate in seclusion; tucked away in a refugium, an animal can temporarily be shielded from predation/aggression in the main tank. More specialized refugia (equipped with tide-simulating plumbing systems) could be used to cultivate salt marsh grasses.

Refugia tend to act as nutrient sinks, trapping and concentrating detritus. A diversity of microbes and small animals consume and fully mineralize the POM as it accumulates. Fast-growing macroalgae (*Ulva*, *Caulerpa*, *etc.*) take up these dissolved nutrients *in situ*, which are ultimately exported from the system when plant biomass is harvested and discarded. It is thought that by aggressively sequestering nutrients, planted refugia compete with, and therefore help to control, undesirable microalgae growth in the main tank.

4. Plumbing

Every plumbing scheme will follow either an open or a closed system design. Basically, open systems continuously pump natural seawater from a nearby shore through an aquarium and then back to the source. Water may be filtered and/or sterilized as it enters and/or exits the aquarium system. The source waters must be unpolluted and of an appropriate, stable temperature and salinity. Typically, seawater quality and consistency will increase with intake depth. Drawing water from below the thermocline and well above the sea floor helps to curb the uptake of sediments and contaminants. However, regardless of the source, the keeper of an open aquarium system is ever at the mercy of every local oil spill, plankton bloom, disease outbreak, heat spell, coastal flood, and so on. There is a comparatively higher degree of control over a properly installed closed

This unusual tank is specially designed to exhibit sea pens. Kenneth Wingerter.

system. Of course, because the same water (aside from the occasional water change or top-off) is continuously recycled through a closed system, it generally must be treated and filtered in some manner to remain hospitable to marinelife. Closed loop plumbing schemes (e.g. sump systems and canister filters) feature a remote pump. The noise and clutter of filter equipment in this situation is expediently removed from the display tank and hidden away elsewhere.

Poor plumbing design results in the need (among other things) for a larger pump, which not only costs more money to purchase but also consumes more electricity and generates more heat, which adds yet more to the ongoing operating expense. Installing a tight, efficient plumbing system often seems easy enough when first setting up an aquarium. But, then, as components get added and stuff gets modified, things can get a lot messier. This is why it is so important to plot your plumbing lines out well from the start. The easier it will be to access, exchange or modify the lines or connected pieces of equipment, the better.

Choice of material will be among the first concerns. Aside from a few exceptions (e.g. titanium), absolutely no exposed-metal plumbing parts can be used, as they rapidly corrode and are often extremely toxic to invertebrates. Most plastic plumbing parts are known to be aquarium safe. Just about all aquarium plumbing systems consist at least partly of polyvinyl chloride (PVC) pipes, hoses, valves, caps and/or fittings.

The popularity of PVC is understandable, given that it is resilient, easy to work with, widely available and relatively inexpensive. A simple, cheap PVC pipe cutter can make very clean cuts without a mess of shavings. Premeasure and draw out the cut line to ensure that cuts are square and precise; make each cut along the outside of each line to allow for sandpapering. Sanding the cut edges will facilitate attachment to fittings and ensure a snug seal. Fittings attach to pipe or each other by way of either slip (S) or threaded (T) connections. The seal is made watertight at the connections with PVC cement (for S or T styles) or Teflon tape (for T styles only). While cement bonds joints very strongly, it is utterly permanent; only taped connections can be broken down and reassembled. Closely follow all given instructions (including safety precautions) when applying primer, cement, tape, etc.

A coldwater marine pond (tidepool?). Kenneth Wingerter.

PVC plumbing parts are available in different classes. The term schedule refers to the wall thickness (i.e. its pressure rating). Schedule 120 is extremely heavy wall, Schedule 80 is heavy wall, Schedule 40 is standard wall thickness and Schedule 20 is light wall. With higher schedule materials, pipe and hose wall thickness increases; the inside diameter (ID) gets smaller while the outside diameter (OD) remains the same. Schedule 120 (which is unnecessarily expensive) and Schedule 20 (which is of an unsuitably low quality) are rarely, if ever, encountered in aquarium applications. Since it is generally of an adequate quality and is very easy to find, Schedule 40 is frequently used by aquarists. However, Schedule 80 is much preferable due to its greater strength and lower rate of heat transfer (even small sections of Schedule 40 plumbing can be prone to sweating in coldwater applications).

Poor planning can result in inefficient plumbing (such as this unnecessary 90° elbow). Note heavy sweating on pipes and tank bottom. Kenneth Wingerter.

Valves can be used to reduce or cut flow through a line as needed. When used to restrict the flow from a pump, place the valve at its outflow, rather than inflow, side. Gate valves, which have a spinning wheel-like handle and sliding gate, are highly adjustable and are resistant to clogging or jamming. Ball valves are relatively inexpensive and are highly portable. Ball valves are sometimes used in conjunction with unions. Unions are a type of coupler that allow for quick connection/disconnection in the plumbing lines and are often useful where certain components (e.g. UV sterilizers) must be removed regularly. Unions are usually flanked by valves that prevent water from spilling out while the union joint is open. Tru-unions are an especially handy fitting that combine a coupling valve with a ball valve. Unions are sealed with an O-ring, which will likely need to be greased and cleaned or replaced from time to time. To avoid messes and potential property damage, prevent leaks by using only the highest quality valves and couplers.

Hose may be used in place of pipe where more tractability is required. The flexibility of PVC hose can provide more freedom when positioning filter components, particularly within the cramped confines of an aquarium stand. It is also preferable for sections of plumbing that are handled frequently (e.g. between a pump and media reactor). PVC hose can be bonded with a special cement directly to PVC pipe. Vinyl hose (clear or tinted) may be alternatively used for many applications. Though not as sturdy or kink-proof as PVC hose, vinyl hose is even more flexible, inexpensive and easy to work with. It can, however stiffen somewhat when cold. Soften stiff vinyl hose ends in boiling water to ease their connection to barbed fittings. There are a number of "quick release" fittings for a few sizes of vinyl tubing that allow for the fast disconnection and reconnection of plumbing lines (e.g. to temporarily remove a canister filter for cleaning). Ribbed flex hose (which is commonly used in pools and hot tubs) is of a durable corrugated construction. Each end has a soft cuff to which fittings can easily be joined. While it might get a little stiff, it will retain its flexibility at lower temperatures than other types. Thus, it is favored in very tight spots (between the drain line and sump under a cabinet) or between frequently serviced (that is, repeatedly moved) pieces of equipment.

Plumbing lines (both return and drain) can pass through openings in the side or bottom of a tank with the use of bulkheads. A bulkhead consists of a threaded body, a gasket and a lock nut. A seal is made by compressing the gasket against the tank panel. The gasket should be on the inside (wet side) of the tank to function properly. Do not overturn the nut, which can distort the shape of the gasket and cause a leak. When sizing a hole for a bulkhead (or vice versa), note that the size given for each fitting refers to its internal diameter.

Return lines lead from the pump (or a battery of pumps) and end with fittings that serve as nozzles, modifying and directing the water current as it enters the tank. Certain specially manufactured plastic return lines made up of interlocking segments of pipe (e.g. Loc-line) can be customized using a motley array of fittings to fine tune water movement. Particularly in larger aquaria, return lines may split and enter the tank from multiple positions. If the end of a return line is submerged deeply, drill a small hole or two into the pipe or hose just below the water surface to ensure that it cannot back siphon when the pump is shut down.

Standing pipes are commonly put into use at the intake end of drain lines. They are generally inserted into a bulkhead fitted into the tank floor. Standpipes should be taped and snugly threaded, rather than glued, into the bulkhead. The constant minimal water level established in an enclosure by a standpipe helps to prevent a total drain of the tank in the event of a pump or power failure. Standpipes are often favored because they draw from the very surface of the water column, which is consequently kept clear of floating debris and oily slicks. Certain styles of standpipe (e.g. Durso standpipes) are modified to reduce the gurgling noise that is generated as water rushes down the drain. Standpipes can be protected and concealed within an overflow compartment. There are usually teeth or slits cut into the top margin of the partition to strain out large floating debris and discourage animal escapes. The standpipe can be cut to any height up to an inch or so below the rim of the tank. Only a small fraction of the tank water volume can (whenever the pump stops running) escape

With double-panel glass sides, a coated steel frame and a built-in filtration/refrigeration system, the Oceanic 55 is an impressive modern take on the classic "classroom tank" design. American Educational Products.

through the drain line if a fully sealed (i.e. watertight) partition is securely in place. In such cases, drain line valves are deemed unnecessary. As they function only through passive (i.e. gravitational) force, drain lines should be of a larger size than the return lines; 3/4 inch return and 1 inch drain lines are commonly used in small to mid-size systems.

Some kind of screen or strainer should cover the intake end of drain lines. This prevents animals from getting sucked up against or going down the drain and keeps debris out of pumps. Do not, however, use mechanical filter media over drains, as these can clog and cause the tank or sump to flood. One example of a very simple strainer consists of a pipe end that is capped and slotted with a small hacksaw. PVC suction screens work quite well over a standpipe or wall-mounted overflow. Screens and strainers must be checked and, if necessary, cleaned daily to prevent blockages.

The most important rule in aquarium plumbing is to keep it simple and secure. Plumbing lines should be as short and tidy as possible; the use of tees and sharp turns (e.g. 90° elbows) should be minimized or eliminated. Use pipes and hose of the correct ID. All of this will reduce friction over the inner surfaces of the plumbing lines, which will allow the pump to operate more efficiently. Use pipe clamps (e.g. Clik-hangers) to tightly fasten any long section of pipe or hose in place. Secure hose connections with hose clamps. Use metal clamps, rather than plastic clamps, whenever possible. Be very careful not to overtighten hose clamps (especially over the cuffs of ribbed tubing). To reduce heat gain, various forms of soft insulation material can be wrapped around and bound tightly to longer sections of pipe and tubing.

5. Pumps, Water Movement and Aeration

If plumbing can be thought of as the blood vessels of an aquarium system, then the pump could only be its heart. Nothing less than a powerful, smartly installed water pump can recreate the dynamic water currents to be found in coastal marine environments. Poor water flow can result in dangerously low dissolved oxygen levels as well as rapid detritus build-up and unwanted algal or bacterial films. Sessile invertebrates will need rather brisk water flow to adequately capture food and expel waste products. It is much better to slightly oversize than to undersize an aquarium pump. Be aware that it is far too easy to overestimate a pump's capacity under real-world conditions.

Use only pumps that are specifically designed for use in saltwater aquaria. To avoid potential contamination, use only air or water cooled, rather than oil cooled, models. Submersible (internal) and non-submersible (external) styles are available. The former are usually water cooled while the latter are usually air cooled. Most aquarium water pumps on the market at this time are magnetically driven centrifugal devices. In this design, a magnet is attached to the impeller shaft assembly, which slips into a small cavity (or volute) inside the pump. On the inside of the pump housing, just under the cavity, is a second magnet. When the pump is running, this internal magnet spins, rotating the other magnet and, along with it, the impeller shaft. Due to the constant grinding, impeller shaft assemblies must be replaced on occasion. Much worse, the resulting friction generates heat. This heat is most readily transferred to the aquarium water by submersible pumps. Hence, at least the larger, main pump(s) should have an external placement. Wherever submersible pumps must be used (e.g. within the main tank for additional circulation), air cooled types that (1) mount just above the tank on brackets or (2) onto a side panel via wet-side (propeller) and dry-side (motor) assemblies (e.g. Vortech) are preferable.

Many marine aquarists are concerned with turnover. Most simply put, turnover is the rate at which the total volume of water in an aquarium passes completely through the life support system (LSS). Open systems will generally demand a lower turnover. Open-system coldwater exhibits at the Seattle Aquarium (Anderson, 2001) operated at a one- to six-hour turnover rate. That is, the total volume of the system is exchanged every one to six hours (smaller systems have higher turnover). For closed aquarium systems, experts often suggest a rate of turnover of as much as ten times the total volume of the aquarium system per hour. Thus, a water flow of approximately 1,000 gallons/hour might be needed for a 100-gallon closed system. From this we can see that a given recirculating system can require a tenfold increase in turnover compared to a similar open system. Still, Moe (1992) suggests a turnover of 3-6 times per hour as a rule-of-thumb, while Delbeek and Sprung (2005) assure us that a turnover as low as 1-3 times per hour might be adequate. As we shall see, the ideal turnover for a particular aquarium depends largely upon the ideal rate of flow through its filter system (and associated components).

The main pump carries out two important, though distinct, functions by (1) circulating water through the filter system and (2) delivering flow within the main tank itself. Oftentimes, the main pump will generate optimal turnover through the filter system but fail to deliver adequate flow (at least everywhere it is needed) within the main tank. In other words, the turnover rate may be sufficient to push lots of water through the filter and maintain excellent water quality, though not provide a strong enough flow within the main tank for certain animals. The main pump should be just large enough to power turnover of the filter system at a maximally efficient flow rate, and so cannot necessarily be relied upon as the sole source of water movement in the main tank.

The main pump is usually positioned beneath the main tank (as with sump systems). This helps to keep the unit primed (i.e. water-filled) whenever the water flow ceases. It also happens to be easier for the pump to push water up than it is to pull it up. Nevertheless, the pump will still have to work against friction and gravity, causing it to operate at a lower efficiency (that is, reduced flow rate). What this means is that one cannot simply install a "1,400 gph pump" on a conventionally plumbed and filtered marine aquarium system and expect the unit to actually deliver anything near 1,400 gph of flow. So, after the plumbing scheme has been laid out, you will need to calculate water velocity losses before going pump shopping.

Large, active, mainly shoaling species (such as *Evistias acutirostris*) require a large, open living space. Ian Skipworth.

Tanks containing potential jumpers (such as this female *Labrus mixtus*) should have a tight lid. Stefano Guerrieri.

Fluid dynamics can be a nebulous subject. However, it is possible to estimate, and consequently account for, the total burden these forces will place on your pump by determining Total Dynamic Head (TDH). In essence, TDH is the difference of head pressure between the inlet and outlet of the pump. It can be described by the simplified formula:

TDH= Static Height + Static Lift+ Friction Loss

where static height (or discharge head) is the distance between the pump and the maximum height of the pipe, static lift (or suction head) is the vertical distance that water must rise before reaching the pump intake and friction loss (or frictional head) is the sum of frictional forces acting against the flow of water. For those who just want to do the math, there are quite a few different, and often fairly complex, equations used to express TDH. For those who seek fast, workable results, good TDH calculators are easy to find online (try http://aquadyntech.com/aqddynamichead.html).

Certain specialized water pumps and adjunctive devices can be used to increase the strength of, and control over, circulation within the main tank. Small submersible pumps (or powerheads) can be placed pretty much anywhere (including the sump or mixing vat) to deliver supplemental water movement to any areas of dead flow. Because of their portability and small size, powerheads can be hidden within the aquascape with reasonable ease. Most, by themselves, are capable only of generating a unidirectional (or laminar) direction of flow. Such will be sufficient when simulating laminar water movement patterns such as oceanic surface currents. In some cases (e.g. simulating subtidal sand flats biotopes), a back-and-forth, bidirectional water flow will be ideal; in other cases (e.g. simulating rocky intertidal biotopes), a chaotic, multidirectional water flow will be ideal. Complicated flow patterns can be created using a battery of powerheads set by

Very strong water flow is required to keep most sessile, azooxanthellate cnidarians (such as *Metridium farcimen*). Daderot.

timers to operate at various intervals. Certain components can be used in conjunction with a pump to simulate wave action. Devices known as wave makers use a special controller (e.g. electronic switching relay) with two or more pumps to generate alternating currents. A similar effect can be produced with a very different device, a sort of switching tee fitting, marketed as the SCWD (or "Squid") valve. Oscillating currents can be generated by top-mounted devices (e.g. SeaSwirl) that deliver flow back and forth across an arc. Pulsing currents can be generated with the use of advanced pumps and controllers that are capable of operating at variable speeds; short pulse wave action generates a back and forth movement (i.e. resonant standing wave), whereas long pulse action generates a flow of water that bounces back from the other side of the tank for complete circulation (i.e. gyre flow). Various types of wave buckets and surge devices can be used (perhaps in rocky shore or beach surf biotope aquaria) to generate stronger, more dramatic wave action. A surge device is basically a vessel, placed above the tank, into which aquarium water is delivered from a pump positioned either in the tank or in some connected reservoir. When the vessel is nearly full, a large pipe rapidly siphons the water back into the tank. This generates a substantial rush of water, often leaving a flurry of air bubbles in its wake. Do not continuously operate wave makers or surge devices; there should be one or more calm periods (that is, reduced wave action) during the day or, most often, at night.

Wrobel (1991) points out that some of the simplest, but most highly effective, means of generating water movement can be applied manually. Broad, wide areas can be swept by hand or with some implement (e.g. wooden spoon). Caves and crevasses can be blown out with a turkey baster. An ordinary plastic pitcher can work well as an improvised, hand-held surge device. All of these methods are useful for lifting deep pockets of detritus and facilitating its subsequent removal. Additionally, the stirring action often elicits a feeding response from some creatures (e.g. barnacles and corals) and can stimulate broadcast spawning in others (e.g. limpets and tunicates).

One of the most important functions of water circulation is to provide aeration. Aeration is best described as the mixing of water with air to replenish O_2 and strip excess CO_2. This mixing is most commonly accomplished through the injection of air into the water column (as with an air pump), by drawing air into a current (as with a venturi apparatus) or by breaking the water up over a medium (as in a trickle filter). Aquarium systems that are fed and/or stocked very heavily can benefit from the use of a degassing column or oxygen reactor. Degassing columns are essentially tall structures that contain inert, high-surface area media. As aquarium water dribbles over the media it is broken up and mixed well with the surrounding air pockets. Degassing towers are fairly simple in design, but necessarily take up much vertical space. Oxygen reactors are comparatively compact and efficient, though a bit more complicated in function. They are usually made up of a sealed and pressurized media-filled chamber. Air is injected directly into the unit. Because of the higher than ambient pressure (around 2-4 psi), the thin film of water over the media is easily saturated with the gas before it is returned to the main tank. Pure oxygen is not always recommended for this purpose due to the potential for toxic supersaturation.

6. Filtration

Over time, aquarium water quality will decline due to the biological activity of the livestock. Optimal conditions cannot be consistently maintained without the support of an aquarium filter system that is appropriately sized and operated at its most efficient flow rate. Even in open systems, water will often need to be filtered to be suitable for sensitive organisms. Different methods of water filtration are employed to remove different kinds of offending substances. Most involve the use of some kind of medium. As a general rule, filter media should have the highest possible amount of surface area and should be placed in an area of high flow where water must pass through, rather than around, the material. The water that passes through a filter medium is referred to as the filtrate. Where effective filtration has been put in place, the filtrate can be recycled many, many times over.

Three basic types of filtration include (1) mechanical, (2) chemical and (3) biological filtration. Mechanical filtration physically strains out large particles onto a permanent or semi-permanent medium, concentrating and holding them in place for trouble-free removal. Proper mechanical filtration virtually eliminates unsightly turbidity. Most importantly, it allows for the quick and easy removal of POM. Water clarity can be greatly improved if POM and other suspended solid wastes are removed from the tank through frequent rinsing of mechanical filter media (that is, before these solid organic materials break down into finer particles). Once trapped, organic particles are rapidly broken down by the action of microorganisms. Mechanical filter media therefore must be washed frequently (daily or even more often if necessary) to prevent the *in situ* decomposition of the trapped particles. Many of these media can be washed and reused for a number of times, but should nevertheless be replaced at the earliest sign of wear.

The size of particle that a mechanical filter medium can capture depends upon its pore size. Common mechanical filter media fiber such as polyester fiberfill sheets and expanded polyurethane foam blocks are usually capable of capturing particles as small as 50-100 microns. Larger aquarium systems may require something with more capacity such as a sand filter. Sand filters trap small (down to 10 microns) particulates in a deep sand bed which is cleaned by routine backflushing. Even more aggressive water polishing can be achieved with the use of diatomaceous earth, which essentially narrows the pores of an existing mechanical filter medium to collect all but the tiniest (down to 2 microns) of particles.

Multiple mechanical filters can be positioned in a series, progressing from coarser to finer media. One popular application involves the combined use of a course filter sock (through which water from the drain line must pass as it enters the sump) and a fine sponge (positioned between the baffles, through which water must pass as it flows through the sump). If it is cleaned frequently, a fiberfill sheet may be laid over the drip tray of a trickle filter. The use of any mechanical filters over drains, in overflow compartments (including the standpipe) or over pump intakes (except those specially made for this purpose) is not recommended.

Intake lines should be covered with a strainer rather than a mechanical filter medium. Kenneth Wingerter.

Chemical filtration removes dissolved pollutants by physically or chemically bonding them—molecule by molecule—onto a disposable medium. Chemical filter media are simply removed and discarded as they are exhausted. Certain chemical filtrants target specific pollutants (ammonia, copper, silicate, etc.) of a particular molecular size and chemistry. Many are of a granular form that can packed into mesh bags, which are then placed in an area of strong flow (safely away from pump intakes) within the sump. Some of these (e.g. granular ferric oxide (GFO)) are best used in a tightly controlled reactor to ensure prime performance. Chemical media are best situated just downstream from the mechanical filter(s); otherwise, they can quickly become smothered in particulates and be rendered ineffective.

Chemical filtration is carried out by way of (1) absorption, (2) adsorption, (3) ion exchange and (4) reverse osmosis. Often, several of these processes take place simultaneously. The simplest form of chemical filtration, absorption, functions more or less like a mechanical filter on the molecular scale. The tiniest molecules can be sieved from the water and locked in the minuscule channels of the media. Unlike absorption, adsorption involves the physical attraction of

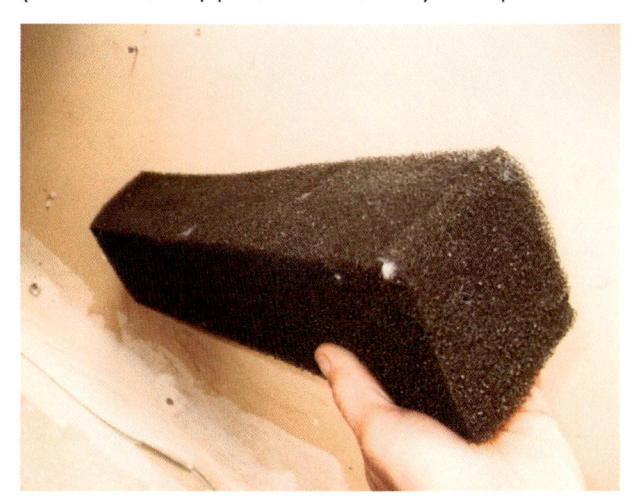

Polyurethane foam blocks fit nice and snugly between sump baffles. Kenneth Wingerter.

Though limited in their capability, air-driven "sponge" filters may be useful in some small tanks containing weak swimmers such as seahorses and jellyfish. Kenneth Wingerter.

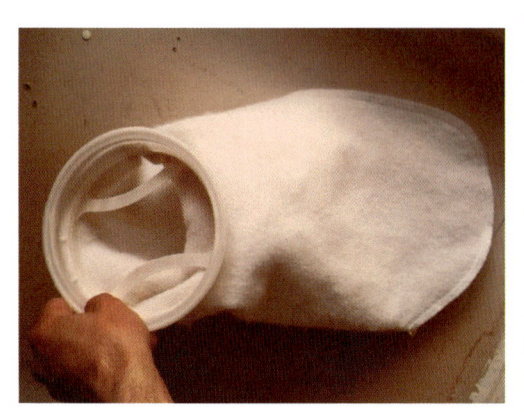

Woven fabric filter "socks" work well as prefilters in sump applications. Kenneth Wingerter.

certain polar molecules to the medium substrate. In a simple process known as solid surface adsorption, molecules (the adsorbates) are locked directly onto the media surface. Of these, activated carbon is surely the easiest and cheapest to obtain. It is consistently effective at removing toxic dissolved organic compounds and metals (e.g. arsenic). It is important to use only "activated" aquarium carbon products, which are specially processed (usually at extremely high temperatures) to produce a high-porosity (that is, high-surface area) material. Passable granular activated carbon (GAC) products have a Total Surface Area (TSA) of at least 500 meters^2/milliliter and a very low ash (i.e. leachable phosphate) content. As much as an ounce of GAC per gallon of system water, replaced (at least) once monthly, might be used in heavily stocked and generously fed coldwater aquaria.

Deionization (DI) removes various harmful or excessive salts from water through ion exchange. Ion exchange is a purely chemical process in which dissolved salts are replaced with hydroxyl (H$^+$) and hydroxide (OH$^-$) ions, which then combine to form water (H$_2$O). DI filter media are styrene-based materials that combine (1) a cationic (i.e. positively charged) resin that is pre-charged with hydroxyl ions and (2) an anionic (i.e. negatively charged) resin that is laden with hydroxide ions. The cationic resins exchange H$^+$ for other positively charged ions (e.g. ammonium) while the anionic resins exchange OH$^-$ for other negatively charged ions (e.g. sulfate). DI resins usually take the form of little beads, which may be specially engineered to remove specific types of molecules. Some of these have color-changing properties that signal the need for replacement. DI media have a longer effective life when preceded by GAC, which helps to protect the resins from chlorine.

Reverse osmosis (RO) removes particles of very small particle size by applying hydraulic pressure to a solution to force it, against solute gradients, through a semipermeable membrane. Only the tiniest molecules (H$_2$O, O$_2$, etc.) can freely pass back and forth across the membrane, effectively excluding many salts and dissolved organics. RO filtration removes contaminants such as silty fines, lead and chloramine. RO membranes have a longer effective life when preceded by a DI filter, which eases high salt loads. Due to the tight, highly restrictive micropore structure of their membranes, RO filters have very limited flow rates (usually measured in gallons per day). They are therefore not to be applied as part of the aquarium life support system, but rather to pretreat freshwater (e.g. tap water) for top-off or for making seawater.

Many solid chemical media function at peak performance for just the first few days of use. Not only can they quickly become exhausted but they are also highly susceptible to clogging by microbial films. A yellowish tinge in the water can serve as a good indication that chemical filtration is inadequate or that the media need to be replaced.

Protein skimming (or foam fractionation) is an adsorptive process that utilizes a gaseous medium (i.e. bubbles). As such, it does not require regular replacement like solid media; the "exhausted" bubbles simply disappear as the foam collapses. While many variations on the basic foam fractionator design exist, it is an instantly recognizable contraption. Most units consist of a tall column topped with a detachable collection cup and dedicated water pump. Air is usually injected into the unit through, and controlled with, an attached venturi valve. Venturis are short air lines plumbed near the outflow of the pump that draw air through their open end when the attached pipe is running with water. A small valve at the open end can be used to control air intake.

Main concerns in maximizing skimming efficiency are (1) air flow rate, (2) bubble size and (3) contact time. Follow manufacturers' guidelines for the optimal air flow rate. In many cases, adjustments to air intake will affect the operating water level in the unit; what often works best is to leave the air valve wide open and then adjust water flow as necessary to produce a rich, dry foam that condenses into a thick, dark liquid. If water or air flow rate is too high, an excessively wet foam will develop, producing a pale, watery liquid. Some assert that overskimming in this manner can lead to the unintentional loss of trace elements. The best results are achieved with the right bubble size. A fairly smallish bubble diameter of around 0.8 millimeters (0.03 inches) is said to be ideal by some, though others suggest smaller sizes. Some models have a needle or pin wheel impeller construction that chops up air that is injected into the pump finely, greatly increasing its exposed surface area.

A clean, properly processed, high-surface area GAC can remove a considerable amount of water-tinting compounds. Pixelmaniac pictures.

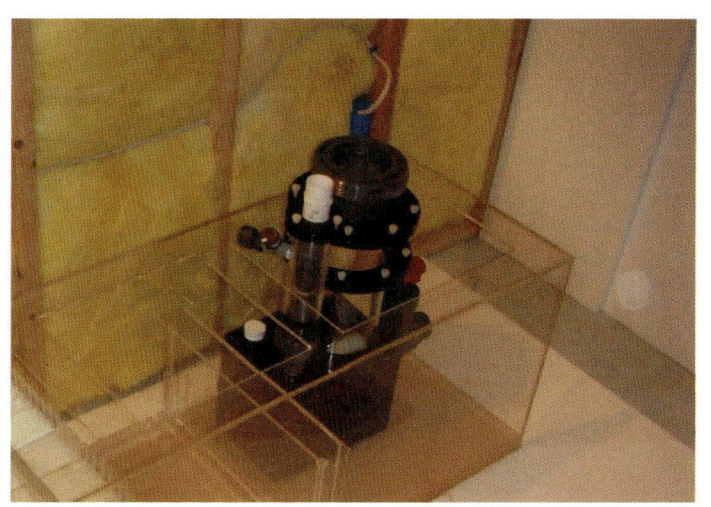

Just as in-sump protein skimmers (such as this one shown with its collection cup removed) conserve cabinet space, they use up valuable sump space; moreover, their submersible pumps can dump extra heat into the system. Gtstricky.

Bubble surfaces are most attractive to surface active agents (or surfactants). Surfactants are molecules that are comprised of a hydrophobic (i.e. repelled by water) terminal and a hydrophilic (i.e. attracted to water) terminal. These substances form a thin layer over each little bubble, with their hydrophobic sides stuck firmly in the gas and their hydrophilic sides projecting in the water. This allows bubbles to retain their shape long enough to amass. Eventually a foam (not unlike the seafoam along a choppy shoreline) builds up at the surface of the water in the column. As it continues to rise, the froth is funneled into the collection cup, where it quickly condenses into a greenish or brownish fluid (or skimmate). The collection cup should be easily removed for cleaning. Installing a drain line from the cup to a larger container (e.g. 5-gallon bucket) can greatly extend the time between cleanings. Protein skimmers can (especially during the "breaking in" period) be finicky gadgets; oily fish foods or even changes in barometric pressure can disrupt their normal function. As such, they should be checked and tweaked often. The different adsorptive properties of protein skimmers and activated carbon are rather complementary to each other; accordingly, in many aquarium systems, chemical filtration is carried out by a combination of foam fractionation and GAC treatment.

Biological filtration involves the use of microbial organisms to remove certain metabolites from aquarium water. The aquarium system should be inoculated with these organisms in earliest stages of successional development. It may be "seeded" in a fairly uncomplicated manner by adding a fresh scoop of sand from a mature, disease-free system. Taking a more targeted approach, one might use some combination of bottled products containing select species or strains of live ammonifying, nitrifying and/or denitrifying bacteria. Different types of bacteria colonize different types of biological filter media. An aquarium system is deemed to be "cycled" when nitrogenous compounds (at least ammonia and nitrite) drop to undetectably low concentrations. The customarily stated purpose of biological filtration is the conversion of highly toxic ammonia to relatively harmless nitrate. In truth, the broader objective should be to develop a dynamic microbial food web that overall promotes a healthy, balanced water chemistry. Such is achieved by cultivating a stable and diverse community of synergetic microorganisms.

A generous amount of high-surface area biological filter media is recommended for coldwater marine systems, where nitrification processes are slowed by the relatively chilly water temperatures. Kenneth Wingerter.

Any nitrifying biofilter media should be composed of a high surface area material. Nitrifying bacteria are ideally cultured on an inert medium (e.g. pea gravel, porous ceramic beads, plastic "bioballs") in an aerobic environment. Foam blocks can function sufficiently as biofilters, so long as they receive enough circulation to maintain an aerobic internal environment and are kept clear of organic films or deposits. Fluidized bed filters, which utilize a deep bed of (usually silica or aragonite) sand grains suspended in an updrafting current, work well for large-scale applications (e.g. aquaculture). Fluidized beds offer an enormous amount of surface area in a relatively small space. One annoying aspect of this method, however, is the tendency for the sand to spill out into the rest of the aquarium system if the unit is malfunctional or improperly adjusted; use of a dedicated prefilter and postfilter will help to contain these sand spills. A more serious drawback is their tendency to rapidly go anoxic if left stagnant (that is, not running) for very long. Wet-dry (or trickle) filtration provides excellent aeration for the culture by allowing the system water to drip over, but not submerge, the biomedia. Because it is not submerged, the medium (so long as it remains wet) will be under little threat of anoxia during short periods of interrupted water flow. Since becoming very popular in the early 1980s, this method has gradually fell out of favor with tropical reef aquarists, who have relied increasingly upon live rock as a primary biological filter medium. All the same, coldwater aquarists, who tend to use stone of a much lower porosity (that is, lower habitable surface area), will benefit greatly from the use of supplemental nitrifying biomedia. As ammonia and nitrite levels drop, there will be a predictable increase in nitrate levels.

Nitrate levels can be maintained below 10 ppm with proper denitrification. While some denitrification will take place in the main tank or refugium (under rocks, in deeper parts of the sand bed, etc.), supplemental nitrate control can be provided with a denitrifying filter. The simplest type of denitrifying filter consists of nothing more than a large foam block, positioned in such a way (usually in the sump) that water flow can freely pass around, but not penetrate and aerate, its interior surfaces. It should be kept clear of heavy POM deposits. In some cases, certain slow-release foods can be inserted into the center of the block to improve its performance. Much more sophisticated flow-through denitrifying filters are available. These are basically media-filled boxes that are completely sealed to air except for a small, one-way valve at the top (to allow for the release of nitrogen gas). Like the nitrifiers, denitrifying bacteria are ideally cultured on an inert medium, albeit in an anaerobic environment. Small water lines run to and from the sump or main tank. A small valve in the line leading from the little pump is used for fine control of water flow. Flow through the unit must be so slow (something like 10-50 milliliters per second) that most of the oxygen is consumed immediately upon entering. The unit should also have some means of adding food (e.g. a sealable tube or door), as the residing microbes are heterotrophic and require a steady source of organic carbon such as lactose or ethanol. If the flow rate (i.e. dissolved oxygen concentration) is too high and/or feeding rate is too low, nitrite can be released; if the flow rate is too low and/or feeding rate is too high, noxious hydrogen sulfide can be released. Owing to their particularity, these filters should be monitored closely. Especially while setting up and establishing a denitrifying filter, it is advisable to frequently test values for pH, nitrite, nitrate and dissolved oxygen concentrations in water flowing to, as well as from, the filter unit. Closely follow any

Plants such as *Chaetomorpha crassa* can be used to sequester excess dissolved nutrients. Daderot.

Canister filters concentrate several types of media into a single remote (albeit less accessible) location. Kenneth Wingerter.

guidelines provided by the manufacturer regarding water flow or feeding rates and carefully make adjusts as necessary.

Carbon dosing is another means of biological nitrate management. Rather than converting nitrate into other compounds (as in denitrification), however, this method uses heterotrophic aerobes to biologically sequester nitrates as well as excess phosphates. A liquid source of fixed carbon (vodka, vinegar, commercial products, etc.) may be used, usually on a daily basis. Dosages of perhaps 5-10 milliliters vodka per 1,000 liters (260 gallons) per day may suffice, depending upon water conditions. Overdoses certainly should be avoided, as the resulting spike in consumption can rapidly deplete dissolved oxygen levels throughout the aquarium system. Though they grow well in the water column, these microbes can be cultured intensely on a solid, biodegradable medium (e.g. pelleted carbon polymers) in an oxygen-rich environment. These media are simply replaced as they are degraded. Special filter components, usually referred to as biopellet reactors, feature an updrafting flow that gently tumbles the medium, keeping it well-aerated and preventing it from clumping. Because these media are consumed in a rather slow, controlled manner, there is little risk of overdosing (as with liquid dosing methods). In theory, nutrient export actually occurs when the bacteria themselves are shed from the aquarium system via mechanical filtration, protein skimming or water changes.

Another form of assimilative nitrate reduction, algae scrubbing, involves the growth of algae on trays or within a special chamber (e.g. A.R.I.D. macroalgal filter). Algal scrubbers generally have a dedicated light source of an ideal intensity and spectral output for the crop species. Heavily planted refugia act as scrubbers, sometimes sequestering enormous amount of nutrients. Biomass of two notably prolific estuarine intertidal macroalgal species, *Enteromorpha prolifera* and *Ulva expansa*, can easily reach a density of 400 grams (dry weight) per square meter. Nutrients are exported from the system when algal biomass is harvested and removed from the scrubber. Algal scrubbing additionally benefits the aquarium system by consuming carbon dioxide, thereby helping to maintain a stable pH. On the other hand, the macroalgae can release copious amounts of yellowing compounds into the aquarium water; these leachates cause an unsightly tinge in the water that can interfere with normal light transmission.

Some aquarium filters are capable of administering mechanical, chemical and biological filtration in tandem. One such "all-in-one" system, the canister filter, basically consists of a sealed container with a pump that shares water

After purification, freshwater can be moved to large containers for storage/mixing. Kenneth Wingerter.

with, but sits below or behind, the main tank. While generally incapable of providing reliable primary filtration for most coldwater marine community aquaria, they can be extremely handy for many small, special or supplemental filtration applications. Canister filters can be easily customized to perform a specific function (e.g. water polishing). They may even be modified into a high-powered DIY aquarium vacuum cleaner (extensions, fittings and all) with a hand-held discharge line that can be used to quickly blow out and mechanically filter large sections of rockwork.

Many outmoded types of aquarium filters ("power" filters, subgravel filters, etc.) remain in the marketplace, usually offered to new hobbyists in beginner's kits. They are incapable of adequately filtering even the smallest of coldwater marine aquaria. As such, a detailed discussion of their function is unwarranted here.

When using seawater that is made from synthetic salt mixes, pretreatment of source waters can ease a major burden on the entire aquarium filtration system. Tap water is not suitable for use in aquaria (including top-off) until it has been properly filtered (before mixing with salt) to remove a host of harmful substances ranging from copper to pesticides. This can best be accomplished only with a quality 4-stage water purification unit. These water purifiers incorporate mechanical filtration (polypropylene sediment cartridge), chemical filtration (carbon block cartridge), reverse osmosis (thin-film composite (TFC) membrane cartridge) and deionization (DI resin cartridge). A good unit will have a total dissolved solids (TDS) readout with filter replacement notification. Some models are capable of performing automatic membrane flushes. Models that feature added protections such as leak detection and automatic shut-off valves can prove to be a worthy investment.

7. Sterilization

Particularly in closed aquarium systems, harmful bacterial/algal blooms or disease outbreaks can quickly overwhelm both aquarium and aquarist. While the complete and permanent elimination of undesirable microorganisms from the system is virtually impossible, an acceptable degree of control can be maintained through the continuous sterilization of aquarium water. Two common methods of sterilization include ultraviolet (UV) sterilization and ozonation.

Ultraviolet light is a form of high-energy shortwave radiation that is potentially harmful to all lifeforms (including humans). Moreover, UV sterilizer bulbs operate at fairly high temperatures (most efficiently at a scorching 40°C (106°F)). Thus, irradiation is made to take place within a protective housing; when sealed, light is not permitted to exit the unit (except maybe through a tiny indicator window). In jacketed styles, the bulb is itself shielded from the water within the housing by a water-tight quartz sleeve. Only jacketed styles should be used in coldwater aquaria; unjacketed styles (which make contact with the water and thereby cool the bulb) yield unacceptably low efficiencies. To avoid overheating and destroying the unit, do not operate it while it is not receiving water flow. Some units include a rather convenient internal brush, enabling the user to wipe the sleeve of light-inhibiting films without having to painstakingly dismantle and reassemble the unit. To avoid loss of efficiency due to turbidity, and to help keep the sleeve clean, the input to the unit should be positioned downstream from filtration (e.g. in a terminal compartment of the sump). To avoid repeatedly re-treating the same water, direct the outflow from the unit downstream (e.g. from the sump to the main tank). The unit should be checked and serviced often; both the bulb and sheath will require regular (ideally scheduled) replacement. Bulbs should be replaced after six months of continuous use; sleeves should be replaced at the first indication of hazing or burning. As quartz sleeves are fairly delicate, they should be handled with care. The use of clean gloves is advised to avoid contamination of the sleeve surface with skin oils, which absorb UV light and reduce the efficiency of the unit.

As aquarium water passes through the unit, the DNA of exposed microscopic organisms is damaged by the high-energy radiation. Many UV sterilizers are designed to emit light of a wavelength of 254 nanometers, well within the optimally lethal range of 240-280 nanometers (UV absorbance of DNA peaks at 260 nanometers). Polychromatic UV lamps (which have numerous peaks of intensity in the lethal range) are better than monochromatic types, as they apparently cause more extensive damage to DNA. Irradiation is measured as the number of microwatts absorbed per square centimeter per second ($\mu W/sec/cm^2$). Irradiation levels of at least 35,000 $\mu W/sec/cm^2$ are recommended for saltwater aquaria. UV sterilization of saltwater occurs at a lower efficiency than that of freshwater, so be sure to rely only on ratings for marine aquaria.

Specific germicidal activity varies between different UV sterilizer models and different modes of operation. A single 9 watt bulb might achieve a satisfactory level of sterilization in a typical 100-gallon system, depending upon the rate of flow. High flow rates yield higher turnover; high intensities kill more of the stuff that passes by. Kill efficiencies are determined primarily by light intensity and contact time (i.e. flow rate). Under a given intensity, a higher contact time is required to kill larger organisms. If the aim is merely to reduce the incidence of water-greening, free-living microalgae (i.e. clarification), the flow rate might be significantly higher than that used to kill relatively huge organisms like parasitic flukes (i.e. true sterilization). A system turnover rate of perhaps once per every couple of hours might be maintained for algae control, whereas the rate maintained to treat a protozoan infestation might be as high as a few times per hour. Thus, even a unit that is operating at a 100% killing efficiency will be limited by the system turnover rate. Since true sterilization requires both high turnover of the system water *and* high irradiation intensity, it can only be achieved using a powerful (and meticulously maintained) UV sterilizer unit. Because UV sterilization kills indiscriminately, the unit should be shut down while adding probiotics, live microfoods, etc.

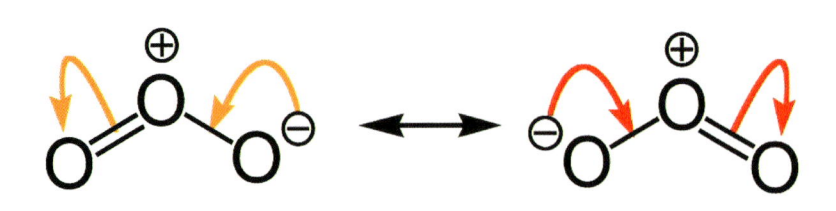

The electrons in an ozone molecule are crowded and easily lost, leading to the decay of O_3 into O_2 as well as the oxidization of organic compounds. Benjah-bmm27.

The most obvious advantage of UV sterilization is its effectiveness against a huge range of bad organisms. Used continuously, it can simultaneously play a major role in disease control and water clarification. Furthermore, unlike many medications, it cannot be overdosed and does not leave any residues behind. Downsides to its use include the potential loss of beneficial microorganisms as well as the added heat input from both the pump and the bulb.

Sterilization can also be achieved with the use of an ozonizer. Contact between ozone and the aquarium water can be enhanced with the use of an oxygen reactor (be sure that it is composed of ozone-safe materials). Ozonation is very effective at killing undesirable microbes, including water-borne parasites. By breaking down DOM, ozonation has additional, beneficial water clarifying effects. It is particularly effective at degrading algal yellowing compounds. A powerful oxidizer, ozone (O_3) damages the living tissues of all living creatures (including humans) and must be handled accordingly. Ozone sterilization can be trickier than UV sterilization to carry out properly. While some aquarists swear by it, others insist that the risks associated with ozonation in closed systems outweigh any benefits. In truth, overdoses can easily result in considerable harm to marinelife (especially invertebrates), so it must be carefully controlled and closely monitored. As a precaution, many aquarists install a GAC reactor (positioned immediately after the ozonizer) to control residual ozone levels. Residual ozone levels of 0.01-0.3 ppm in the main tank will inhibit the growth of bacteria (the good along with the bad) and can injure some invertebrates. Even at these seemingly low doses, prolonged exposure can kill many aquarium animals. Making matters worse, precisely testing ozone levels in the aquarium water (at least using methods available to the average aquarist) is not easy. A rough figure can be obtained using an orthotolidine (OTO) based chlorine test kit. A more reliable way to keep track of residual ozone levels is indirectly through the use of a redox monitor.

When first operating an ozonizer, start with a safe, low dosage (0.003-0.005 milligram/liter/hour). The initial dose should be increased only very slowly (over days or weeks) until the desired results are achieved. Then, you may even have to back off a bit once most of the DOM build-up has been broken down. A dosage of 0.5 mg/L/hr might be adequate for a larger, highly stocked fish-only system, though one might not wish to exceed a dosage 0.05 mg/L/hr for any system containing sensitive invertebrates. Check for the presence of ozone in the main tank following any sudden reduction of organic load (when replacing GAC, performing large water changes, etc.), which potentially permits excess ozone to leach into the main tank. If residual ozone is detected in the main tank, or if there is the faintest hint of an ozone odor in the open air, shut the unit down immediately. When all traces of ozone are gone, resume operation at a reduced output (perhaps 50%). Continue to test the main tank waters for residual ozone. If you must be away from the tank for an extended period of time, or for any other reason cannot monitor ozonation closely, it is best to be precautious and temporarily shut the unit down.

8. Temperature Control

Temperature control is one of the most important functions of the aquarium life support system. If it must be said, coldwater marine aquaria need to be kept cold. Most cold-adapted marine species experience significant stress when exposed even briefly to water temperatures above 18°C (65°F). Thus, any recirculating coldwater aquarium system should include a powerful, reliable aquarium refrigeration unit (usually referred to as a chiller). These pressurized refrigeration units work in a way that is similar to a typical kitchen fridge. They usually utilize some chlorofluorocarbon (e.g. Freon), though some eco-friendly models are now available. A small compressor within the unit pushes the coolant through a long, thin metal tube. The coolant is pumped to a condenser where it compressed into a liquid under high pressure. This causes it to release heat, which is ultimately transferred to, and expelled with, the air flow. The coolant then moves on through an expansion valve where it vaporizes under the greatly reduced pressure. This causes it to absorb heat from the aquarium water through a thermally conductive and aquarium-safe titanium heat exchanger. It is subsequently directed back towards the compressor where it is recycled.

Chillers are available in drop-in and in-line styles. Drop-in styles, which have a titanium coil that can be dropped directly into the main tank or sump, do not require a water pump and are a bit easier to install. On the other hand, they must be inspected often to be sure that the seals around the fittings of the coolant lines remain tight. In-line models are a little more affordable and are much more common. Water moves through in-line units in a titanium heat exchanger that is tucked within the housing of the unit. These heat exchangers receive water flow from the main pump or from a dedicated pump. A dedicated pump is preferable, as it allows for better control over flow rates. This pump must run whenever the chiller is on. If the chiller must be plumbed into the return line (in other words, without its own pump), then put it at the end of the line after UV sterilization. This will control biofouling within the chiller's water lines (which can clog pipes and impact flow rates) as well as enable the unit to handle heat dumped by the sterilizer. To save space and ease maintenance, some chiller models now integrate a UV sterilizer. Whatever style of chiller you use, closely follow the manufacturer's recommendations for minimum and maximum flow rates.

Aquarium refrigeration is controlled by a thermostat. Most chiller designs now integrate a microchip thermostat into the unit. You should be able to designate two set points—a high temperature point that will trigger operation and a low point that will shut it down—as to prevent the unit from shutting off and on relentlessly (or short-cycling).

There is no way around it; though they have become more efficient over the years, aquarium chillers can consume a good deal of electricity. Good insulation, smart plumbing, etc. will help to keep operating costs low by reducing operating time. Though it may seem counterintuitive, a larger unit will consume less energy than a smaller one to cool the same aquarium owing to its better work efficiency. Additionally, a slightly oversized unit will allow for the installation of additional equipment, go the extra mile on unusually hot days, etc. Still, if it is overly oversized, it can short-cycle, leading to needless wear on the unit. Chiller models that are specially manufactured for coldwater (rather than tropical) applications will yield the highest efficiencies.

You first need to know how much heat you will have to remove from the system to reach your target water temperature. This can only be estimated, as there are numerous factors from both inside and outside of the aquarium system that will influence the chiller workload. Heat that will be added by lights, pumps, etc. must be accounted for. Perhaps the most reliable way to determine the necessary chiller size for a given application is to actually run the entire, fully constructed system on a warm day minus any refrigeration. The number of degrees between the maximum operating water temperature and the target water temperature is referred to as the pull-down. This number can be plugged into a chiller sizing chart along with system water volume to provide a suggested chiller size. Chiller sizes are given in watts, except in North America, where they are usually given in horsepower (HP). One horsepower is equivalent to 3,517 watts. Note that this number is a measure of cooling capacity rather than electrical consumption of the unit. Generally, cooling effect is 1-3 times greater than power consumption. Hemdal (2006) provides a rule-of-thumb for quick sizing estimations, reckoning that a 15-20 degree F pulldown can be achieved in an adequately insulated 75-gallon system with a 1/6 HP unit and in a 700-gallon system with a 3/4 HP unit.

Temperature readings should be taken directly from the tank as well as from the chiller unit. Stu Wobbe.

Even an oversized chiller will scarcely have an effect on the aquarium water temperature if the heat it extracts is dumped right back into the tank. This is exactly what will occur if the hot air is exhausted near the aquarium system. For this reason, it is often preferable to move the chiller to a remote, well-ventilated area. Get the hot air as far away from the area as possible; if it continues to recycle through the unit, it will draw very little heat from the coolant. For this reason, a chiller should never, ever be crammed inside of a poorly ventilated tank cabinet. Even a small room can quickly heat up due to the normal activity of a working chiller. Thus, the building (or at least the room that the chiller is in) should be properly climate controlled with an air temperature well below 35°C (95°F). Place it on the floor to ensure that it draws the coolest air in the room. If the unit is enclosed in a sound-dampening cabinet, be sure that it is fanned and ventilated well.

Small, thermoelectric aquarium refrigeration units have been in use for some time now. This technology uses a special circuit to make one side of an element hot and the other cold. Only the cold side comes into contact with the aquarium water; the hot side communicates with a heat sink from which thermal energy is radiated into the air. Though they are (as advertised) very quiet and efficient, they are only capable of a pulldown of a few degrees below ambient temperatures. They are thus unsuitable for coldwater applications unless multiple units are used, in which case they are a rather uneconomical choice. The many versions of the DIY minifridge chiller are similarly ineffective. By all reports from those who have actually used them, they are far too weak to adequately service a coldwater aquarium and deserve no further mention here.

Fans and heat sinks should be cleared of dust and debris regularly. Kenneth Wingerter.

Workload on the chiller can be reduced by utilizing good insulation and passive cooling. Insulation materials that will not degrade or compact when wet are best. Foam- or rubber-based thermal insulation material with a closed-cell structure (e.g. Styrofoam) can be applied over tank panels and plumbing. Insulating electrical equipment in this manner, however, cannot be recommended as it poses a fire hazard. When using adhesive insulation materials, finish the application before operating the refrigeration unit to avoid incomplete adhesion to the surfaces due to condensation.

Aquarium cabinetry should have vents (preferably with fans) if it encloses any heat-generating equipment. Much heat can be eliminated simply by installing the life support system (pumps, UV sterilizer, chiller, etc.) in a cooler area of the building such as a basement or shaded garage. Though the effect of evaporative cooling is greater in tropical aquaria, it can nevertheless have a considerable impact on water temperature in coldwater systems. It can take place on the surface of trickle filter media as well as the air-water interface in the main tank and sump. Because this occurs even if the temperature of the water is lower than that of the air, it is possible for the cooling effect to counteract gains from direct air-to-water heat transfer. Fans can be used to enhance surface water evaporation. They are, of course, seen and heard less when placed over the sump (that is, within the cabinetry). However, there are certain benefits to placing a fan over the main tank. For example, in this position, it can serve additional, valuable purposes such as blowing away heated air from the light fixtures and generating "wind-driven" surface currents within the tank. Some modern aquarium cooling fans (e.g. Teco E-Chill) are so efficient and controllable that they blur the line between active and passive cooling.

9. Lighting

It is often said that lighting is not an important consideration for coldwater aquaria. Nothing could be further from the truth. In actual fact, it can be downright crucial that light conditions are properly simulated. Realistically simulating natural light conditions (e.g. seasonal variation) for these systems can be rather challenging. There are a great many kinds of coldwater aquaria, and the light conditions required by each differ considerably with respect to (1) intensity, (2) character and (3) photoperiod. The best choice of lighting depends primarily upon the sort of environment to be represented.

There are many types of lighting (incandescent, fluorescent, metal halide, LED, etc.) that have been developed over the years. These all vary in efficiency, generating different ratios of heat and emitted light. It is this efficiency that should be of greatest concern to coldwater aquarists. Total light output of the light source is divided by the total power input, with efficacy expressed in output per watt. Any "wasted" wattage is converted into thermal energy. For this reason, wattage-per-gallon is an ill-chosen (if not totally senseless) guideline for sizing an aquarium light.

Intensity (or irradiance) is usually a main concern in aquarium lighting selection. Intensity describes the "brightness" of a light source in terms of the number of photons (usually in micromoles (μmol), or parcels of 602 quadrillion) striking a given amount of surface per some unit time. Mean light intensity depends primarily upon latitude. Surface sunlight intensities often exceed 2,000 μmol/m^2/sec along the equator. While intensities in the mid-latitudes can approach this value during the midsummer months, they are typically around half of that. This, of course, drops sharply with increasing depth, turbidity and overcast. Because many temperate marine photoautotrophs are adapted to dim, murky conditions, a bottom light intensity of 20-40 μmol/m^2/sec at 10-12 hours per day is generally sufficient to cultivate low light-adapted flora such as subtidal red macroalgae.

Some deep-water systems will require no supplemental lighting at all. Indeed, these aquaria can suffer from an unusual problem: light pollution. Consequently, they should never be set up in an area of bright ambient light. Just a little bit of unwelcome illumination can disturb the natural behavior (e.g. foraging activities) of many deep-water fishes. It can also cause algal fouling that would compromise any attempt to plausibly simulate a naturalistic deep-water benthic community. Wherever unlit aquaria pose problems for viewing, supplemental red light (which is not visible to most deep-water dwellers) can be used. Anything from hand-held red flashlights to submersible red spotlights can be used for this purpose.

Kelvin (K) temperature ratings are used to characterize the perceived color of light emitted by a particular source, ranging from red at the lower end to blue at the higher end. Photosynthetically active radiation (PAR) encompasses the spectral range of light wavelengths that can be utilized by photoautotrophs (400-700 nanometers), most often falling somewhere from 6,500-10,000 K. PAR is expressed as μmol of photosynthetically active photons/m^2/sec, a measure of photosynthetic photon flux density (or PPFD). Aquaria representing shallow water habitats require especially strong, full-spectrum (that is, "white") light of around 6,500-7,100 K. Aquarium lighting units such as those designed to culture tropical stony corals are ideal for this application, particularly if intertidal seaweeds or zooxanthellate cnidarians (e.g. *Anemonia viridis* and *Anthopleura xanthogramma*) are to be kept. A bluer light (7,100-10,000 K) can be used for shallow subtidal biota but should be similarly intense, particularly if kelps are to be kept. Subdued, predominantly blue lighting (10,000-20,000 K) should be used when recreating deeper habitats.

The daily light cycle of most advanced aquarium systems is controlled by some type of timer. This may range from simple house light timers from the hardware store to much more advanced gadgets, often built into the unit, that are capable of replicating sunrises/sunsets, lunar cycles and even random weather events. Temperate aquaria will do best (or will at least be a lot more authentic and interesting) if daily light cycles are manipulated to simulate seasonal changes in day length throughout the year. While incremental changes are probably better, it may be enough to adjust the light cycle four times yearly (with the passing of each solstice and equinox). The light cycle of a refugium may differ from that of the main tank. Often, the two alternate between 12-hour cycles. This is done to stabilize heat input from the lighting fixtures. Alternating light cycles in this way can also help to balance the consumption of CO_2 by primary producers and thus stabilize the pH throughout the daily cycle.

LED spotlighting can look pretty good. Kenneth Wingerter.

At present, the consensus among experienced coldwater aquarists is that light-emitting diode (LED) lighting fixtures are best. In addition to having a high efficiency, they are compact, exhibit excellent economy of operation and are highly controllable. They do not utilize expensive light bulbs that must be regularly replaced. And, they dump comparatively less heat into the system. Though other lighting technologies such as fluorescent and metal halide lights remain in the marketplace, they are (especially as the base cost of quality LED units drops) quickly becoming antiquated like the incandescent styles of not so long ago.

Most good LED aquarium light models are now capable of moonlight simulation. Many aquarists enjoy a little illumination for nocturnal viewing. But moonlights can also promote the natural early-morning/late-evening (e.g. crepuscular) activities of some species. Furthermore, they can provide a sense of nighttime security for skittish species such as seadragons. They are especially useful for simulating the 29.5-day lunar light cycle. Some suggest programming the operation of these lights to match the actual lunar cycle. Lunar cycles (which coincide with the cycle of tides) serve to regulate the metabolic and reproductive activity of many species. However, care should be taken to avoid using excessive "moonlight," which can easily disrupt the normal nighttime behavior of more secretive species. To be sure, it is pretty easy to overdo moonlight intensity. Even the brightest full moon (which is tens of thousands of times weaker than the Sun) will in the clearest conditions deliver no more than 0.05 µmol/m²/sec. For this reason, even a single blue one-watt LED moonlight can be excessively intense. It has been said that if you can read by your moonlight, it is too bright. Moreover, moonlights should be of an appropriate color. Despite the preponderance of bluish moonlights out there, real lunar light (despite its silvery appearance to our eyes) is actually a bit redder than noontime sunshine, peaking at 643 nanometers.

Point source lighting such as LED (as opposed to diffuse lighting such as fluorescent) can produce flashes of light known as ripple lines over the aquarium bottom. This results from the diffraction of light as it passes through wavelets at the water surface. The effect is magnified with increased surface agitation. Many aquarists find the effect natural looking and aesthetically pleasing. Still, one should be aware that the increased diffraction and reflection of light at the surface can reduce light penetration by as much as 30%. It is therefore advisable to compensate for this if the surface waters will be strongly agitated by fans, wavemakers, dump buckets, etc.

In addition to ripple lines, light penetration can be significantly reduced through absorption in the presence of excessive POM, yellowing compounds, plankton, etc. These and other factors make precisely calculating light intensities within various parts of the aquarium quite difficult. The use of a simple, inexpensive hand-held photometer with an underwater sensor can help with this task. If there is any doubt that a particular light will provide adequate intensity, it is advisable to purchase an oversized unit and dim it as necessary. This is not really wasteful, as running the unit under full power may significantly extend its life.

10. Electrical Systems

Saltwater and electricity are a dangerous mix. A typical marine aquarium system has a considerable amount of electrical components with wires only millimeters away from mishap. Aquarists have lost their lives working on tanks with electrical problems. It is fair to say that electrical safety may be the only concern that is greater than the health of the aquarium inhabitants. Good planning and regular inspection can significantly reduce the risk of deadly shocks and fires. Placement of the aquarium itself is a primary consideration here. Due to the inevitable escape of moisture, it can prove a mistake to place it too near an electrical outlet. Connection to the outlet can be made remotely with a heavy-duty extension cord. The cord connections can be protected with a special weatherproof cover. Cords on components can be kept tidy with a cable organizer. Cords should droop slightly below the outlets or pieces of dry equipment that they lead to, creating what is known as a drip loop. Any water that might run down the cord will trickle at the loop, thereby preventing contact with the component or power source. If a tank or sump absolutely must be in close proximity to a power source, the outlet should be protected with a weatherproof receptacle cover and inspected frequently.

Sweating, splashes, spills and overflows will happen from time to time (for some of us, all of the time). In these situations, if there is a tangled web of cords and power strips shoved behind the tank, serious accidents can occur. The power strips simply must be in a permanently dry location. They are ideally secured in an area well above the aquarium (e.g. suspended from the ceiling) or tightly fastened to the wall over the tank. Power strips should be kept clean of any crusty salt accumulations (or salt creep). A tight-fitting lid should be put in place if any discernable amount of spray is released from the tank or sump. Sometimes, despite the best efforts of the aquarist, water can find its way to an electrical current. Stray voltage can be generated from heaters, pumps, lights, and other pieces of equipment inside and outside of the aquarium. When the aquarium water is "lit up" it is dangerous to both the animals and their keepers. If one encounters any suspicious burning odors or a telltale tingling feeling while working in the tank, be sure to immediately unplug all devices in and near the aquarium system before touching anything else. Wear shoes and avoid standing in wet areas on the floor. A simple, cheap titanium grounding probe can divert and remove stray electrical currents and thus prevent some very unfortunate experiences. All aquarium electrical systems should be GFI protected. If a piece of electrical equipment shows any sign of damage, discard it immediately.

Sooner or later, an aquarist will have to deal with a power outage. Without electricity to power the pumps and life support system, livestock will be increasingly stressed with each passing minute. For obvious reasons, summertime outages in warmer regions are especially threatening. As your investment in livestock grows, you might strongly consider protecting it by obtaining a back-up power source. Back-up power can be supplied by a generator. The size of generator will, of course, be determined by the normal consumption of the aquarium system. Certain devices used as power back-ups for computers (e.g. EatON 5S1000LCD) are affordable, portable and provide a reasonable measure of protection for modestly sized aquaria. They are small enough that multiple units can be added for extended coverage. Battery-powered air pumps can provide additional precious surface agitation and deep circulation during a power failure. These devices are nevertheless incapable of independently supporting a typical aquarium in the event of an extended outage. As such, they can only be considered to be supplementary to devices such as generators.

11. Aquascaping

Aquascaping can be one of the most fun and personally rewarding activities for an aquarist. Even in purely utilitarian holding systems, keepers may feel the very human inclination to arrange items within the tank in an aesthetically pleasing manner. That being said, aquascaping can also be one of the most challenging tasks. This so because the objective is less about decorating and more about creating an ideal living environment for the aquarium inhabitants. The more diverse a given livestock list is, the more complicated it will be to provide suitable microhabitats for all. Most aquarists will have some idea as to what kinds of flora and fauna will be kept, which will dictate what sort of environment will be required, which will determine what aquascaping materials will be used. The framework of many aquascapes consists of some combination of larger rocks (i.e. the hardscape) and a sand or gravel bottom. A rocky intertidal theme will require the copious use of stone and little (if any) soft substrate, whereas an estuarine mudflat will need a deep, fine, soft substrate and minimal rockwork. Pretty much any type of material can be used so long as it is chemically inert in saltwater.

Perhaps aside from the creatures themselves, it is the stonework that most readily distinguishes a coldwater from a tropical reef aquarium. While the latter is more or less restricted to chunks of calcium carbonate accreted by corals and other organisms, the former can include a very wide variety of materials. This certainly might include reef rubble, particularly if one is attempting to recreate the deep-water environments that are adjacent to coral reefs. But most types of igneous and sedimentary forms of stone will do as well. Rocky reef shores in temperate regions are composed of granite, sandstone, limestone and/or shale. This broad selection of hardscaping materials helps the builder to create a more unique and customized display. Many will, if possible, obtain stone composed of a material that is prevalent in the animals' natural habitat. Better still is so-called live rock, which is stone that has been colonized (usually in the natural environment) by various microbes, encrusting algae and small sessile invertebrates.

Stacking the rocks requires some care. If they fall, they can injure animals, damage equipment or even break the tank. Various aquarium-safe epoxies and putties can be useful for securing small chunks here and there, but cannot be trusted to hold larger pieces of heavy stone (e.g. basalt). It should go without saying that no rock should be placed in a way that it could easily loosen and tumble. For those who wish to lighten the load of

Treated wood structures can add visual interest to a display. Kenneth Wingerter.

For safety, wet labs (such as the Aquarium Science Program Building, here shown under construction) suspend electrical cords well above the floor. Kenneth Wingerter.

the hardscape (and perhaps promote the growth of certain beneficial microbes), it is possible to build upon a base composed of a light-weight, porous stone (lava rock, coral skeleton, etc.). A load may be similarly lightened (and nice, habitable caves created) with the use of a sturdy eggcrate or fiberglass grate platform on a PVC frame. The shelves of the platform can be completely hidden beneath the outer rockwork.

One might forego the use of natural stone altogether, opting for an artificial hardscape formed from polyurethane foam or certain resins. Before the artificial rockwork cures, natural sand and grit can be worked into its surface to create a more realistic texture. In time, as it becomes covered with marinelife, it can be virtually indistinguishable from the real thing.

The bottom substrate can likewise be of varied composition. A deep-water Atlantic theme might include an ultra-fine silica-based mud or sand whereas a deep-water Pacific theme might use a dark, basaltic sand with sprinkles of aragonite grit. Temperate themes generally use gravelly aggregates of decomposed (i.e. weathered) granite, but really anything from silt to shell hash may be used, depending upon the type of habitat to be recreated. Substrate depth may be just enough to cover the bottom or, if housing infaunal organisms, be several inches deep. Some aquarists, under the notion that it collects and stores detritus, choose to use no substrate at all. While there may be some truth to this assumption, by totally eschewing a substrate one may also be depriving the system of an important means of biological waste management. Thus, an aquarium system with a bare-bottom display tank can benefit from the presence of a deep sand bed (DSB) by adding a few inches or more of fine, mineral-rich substrate (e.g. Miracle Mud) to the bottom of the refugium. So-called live sands can add a variety of beneficial microbes (and sometimes even interesting infaunal hitchhikers) to the system.

Certain types of wood may be used effectively in coldwater aquaria. Beachwood can enhance the appearance of a salt marsh or sandy shores aquarium. Sections of wooden poles can persuasively suggest pier pilings. Beaten timber can be made to look like the flotsam of a wrecked ship. One should be aware, though, that wood materials can leach substances that might discolor the water and/or lower the pH. To prevent this (as well as rot), the material can be pre-treated with a heavy coat of clear polyurethane.

Choice of background can dramatically affect the feel of an aquascape. Some (as when the tank is oriented in a wing position) elect to use no backdrop at all, leaving a clear, unobstructed view completely through the tank. In most cases, a black, grey or blue background is painted onto the back of the rear tank panel. The impression of vast, open waters in the background can be created by backlighting the rear panel with a diffuse light source. In this case, the back of the tank may be covered with one or more sheets of bluish translucent acrylic and lit from behind. Of course, this will only produce a convincing illusion if no tubing, cords or equipment are there to cast shadows. Cut or molded internal backdrops serve a similar purpose and can additionally help to conceal eye sores by smoothing out corners, covering tank seams, etc. One drawback to this approach is the need to keep the backdrop surfaces completely free of fouling organisms. An array of plastic films can be externally applied to the tank panels for multiple purposes. For example, where predominantly blue light is used for deep-water applications, blue-filtering films can be applied to the front panel (or part of it); this enhances viewing by imparting a true-color (that is, surface color) appearance to the tank interior.

A rocky reef aquascape dominated by large South African sea anemones. Vberger.

Increasingly, wet labs and "mini-aquariums" are being constructed to educate, as well as entertain, the public. Kram-bc.

V. Aquarium Hygiene/Water Quality
1. Basic Parameters

Natural seawater is an aqueous solution that contains around 3½% (by weight) dissolved substances. The chemical makeup of seawater is fairly uniform across the Ocean. Sea salts include all inorganic materials that remain when seawater is evaporated. There is approximately 965 grams of pure water and 35 grams of salt in every kilogram of seawater. Roughly 86% of sea salt (by weight) is made up of sodium chloride. The remaining 14% includes just about every other known element. By proportion, the most common elements include chloride (55.07), sodium (30.62), sulfate (7.72), magnesium (3.68), potassium (1.10) and bicarbonate (0.41). Although sodium chloride makes up the bulk of sea salt, there is a considerable number of minor and trace elements present. Some of these lesser constituents (the so-called nutrient salts) are known to be essential for most forms of life. It is important to note, however, that not all trace elements are essential.

While every synthetic seawater recipe varies a little in some respect, most closely match natural seawater chemically. It is, in fact, near perfect when mixed with pure water. But, after having been altered through the many biological activities within the aquarium system, seawater degrades in quality. Certain water chemistry parameters therefore must be closely watched. Imbalances are best corrected as soon as they are detected. The most important (but certainly not only) parameters to monitor are salinity, pH, alkalinity, calcium, magnesium, potassium, iodine, ammonia, nitrite, nitrate, phosphate, silicate, iron, dissolved oxygen and ORP.

Salinity is probably the most frequently tested parameter for marine aquaria. Salinity is a measurement of the total dissolved salt concentration in seawater. This measurement is commonly expressed as parts per thousand (ppt), as practical salinity units (psu) or as specific gravity (S.G.). Salinity in ppt is simply defined as the number of grams of dissolved solids per liter in seawater (ppt and grams per liter (g/L) are pretty much equivalent). Units in psu reflect the ratio of conductivity of a water sample relative to that of a standard solution of potassium chloride (a salinity of 35 psu is very close to that of 35 ppt). Most commonly, aquarists measure salinity in terms of specific gravity. Specific gravity is the density of a liquid sample relative to that of pure freshwater at the same temperature. Because salt concentration has a predictable impact on water density, salinity can be calculated from specific gravity by extrapolation. Some aquarists use a hydrometer to measure salinity. Hydrometers of various designs all use some kind of floating device to obtain a value for the seawater's density to yield a result in S.G. A temperature compensated refractometer will yield slightly more accurate results. Refractometers use the degree of refraction of light through a water sample to determine water density at room temperature, which is used to calculate salinity, which is expressed generally as specific gravity and sometimes as parts per thousand. Due to their much greater precision, aquarists are increasingly relying on digital salinity meters.

One of the most frequently tested water parameters is pH. Essentially a measure of hydrogen ion (H^+) content, pH is given as a number between 0 and 14 (where 7 is neutral), indicating whether a solution is acidic (<7.0) or basic (>7.0). It is a logarithmic scale, meaning that each value is ten times stronger than the value that preceded it. A lower number in the scale signifies a larger hydrogen ion concentration. Thus, a pH of 2 is ten times more acidic than 3 and is a hundred times more acidic than 4. Water (H_2O) molecules readily break and reassemble as hydrogen ions (H^+) and hydroxide ions (OH^-). In absolutely pure water, the pH is 7.0 (that is, neutral) because there is an equivalent number of hydrogen and hydroxide ions present.

Seawater is mildly basic. Generally, pH values of 8.0-8.4 are acceptable in marine aquaria, though 8.3 is generally ideal. Many of the substances that tend to build up in closed systems (i.e. acids) increase hydrogen ion concentrations, gradually lowering pH values over time. Because hydroxide molecules react with hydrogen ions to form water, low pH values can be remedied with the addition of a base. Strong bases such as calcium hydroxide ($Ca(OH)_2$) work quickly and reliably for this purpose, but must be used incrementally and in small quantities as to not shock the aquarium inhabitants. Calcium hydroxide is usually added with top-off water (it must be prepared in pure freshwater) as a super-saturated solution known as limewater or kalkwasser. Carefully follow the manufacturer's instructions for preparation and use, as kalkwasser is very caustic and can harm aquarium specimen and aquarist alike.

The capacity of an aqueous solution to neutralize acids is referred to as alkalinity. Total alkalinity (A_T) is a measurement of all bases in the water. The carbonate alkalinity (A_C) is only that part of total alkalinity that consists of bicarbonate and carbonate base. Carbonate forms account for over 95% of total alkalinity. Thus, the stability of the pH of seawater is strongly influenced by carbonate and bicarbonate ion, the former being most responsible for the stabilizing effect. Alkalinity is typically given as mg/L, which can be converted into milliEquivalents per liter (mEq/L) by dividing by 50. Aquarists usually give carbonate alkalinity as KH, which is often measured in degrees (dKH) instead of mg/L $CaCO_3$. One dKH equals 17.9 mg/L. Carbonate alkalinity should be around that of natural seawater (7-10 dKH). Since carbonate alkalinity is quickly neutralized in closed systems by biological waste products, some aquarists compensate for the rapid depletion by slightly bumping up the carbonate alkalinity to 9-12 dKH. This not only leaves plenty of carbonate available for organisms that need it, but it also provides a greater buffer against changes in pH and alkalinity, thereby increasing its "buffering capacity." Sodium bicarbonate ($NaHCO_3$), otherwise known as baking soda, can

Stony corals such as *Balanophyllia europaea* require proper calcium levels for long-term survival. Parent Géry.

be used as a buffering agent. Sodium "bicarb" should only be used when the pH reaches the low end of the acceptable range. It should be thoroughly dissolved in purified water before being added to the aquarium. Each teaspoon of baking soda per 25 gallons of system water should increase the pH around 0.1 unit. Avoid changes in pH that are greater than 0.1 unit per day. Be very careful to avoid overdosing carbonate buffers, as they can (among other bad things) precipitate out with (and thus deplete) important minerals such as calcium.

Calcium ion (Ca^{2+}) concentrations should be similar to those in the ocean—something like 400 ppm. Calcium plays a major role in balancing the pH-carbonate system. Calcium levels should be monitored regularly, as they can become greatly diminished over time. Calcium loss takes place through spontaneous and biological precipitation. The potential for depletion due to biological activity is especially high in closed systems that have an abundance of calcium carbonate-secreting cnidarians (e.g. *Stylaster*, *Astrangia*), molluscs (e.g. *Mercenaria*) or hard algae (e.g. *Phymatolithon*, *Lithothamnion*). Calcium chloride ($CaCl_2$) can be used to restore calcium levels where the pH is optimal. Kalkwasser might serve as a better calcium supplement where the pH needs to be slightly increased. Because calcium is more soluble at lower temperatures, coldwater organisms have more difficulties precipitating it, and may consequently substitute a significant amount of it with strontium. Thus, the strontium level (ideally around 8.0 ppm) should be monitored closely along with that of calcium.

Magnesium is also commonly associated with calcium, to which it is chemically similar. It also plays a significant role in the overall mineral balance of seawater, as it reduces the rate at which calcium carbonate precipitation occurs. It is the third most abundant ion and the second most abundant positively charged ion in seawater. Magnesium concentration averages around 1,280 ppm in seawater, though it varies significantly with changes of salinity. Magnesium ions can be replenished in closed systems as needed with the addition of magnesium sulfate and/or magnesium chloride salts.

Despite its importance, potassium (K^+) is not regularly monitored by many marine aquarists. Potassium is regarded as an important macronutrient for plants. It is also associated with the pigmentation of some cnidarians. It is a component of aragonite, and so is part of the skeletons, shells and spicules of countless marine species. Potassium should be maintained at a concentration of 380 ppm. It can be replenished with the use of potassium sulfate and/or potassium chloride.

Iodine is necessary to maintain exoskeleton health in crustaceans such as this *Betaeopsis aequimanus*. Graham Bould.

Iodine (including both organic and inorganic forms) can be found in natural seawater at a concentration of about 0.06 ppm. Iodine appears to be an essential nutrient for many red and brown macroalgae (e.g. *Polysiphonia*, *Ectocarpus*). Soft corals (e.g. gorgonians, sea whips) incorporate significant quantities of iodine into their bodies. Crustaceans (e.g. shrimp) are believed to need it to properly shed and replace their exoskeletons. It has been found to play a role in the immunological response of some fishes. Iodine may be rapidly taken up by organisms in the aquarium and might be further removed through chemical filtration. However, supplementation is not always necessary if plenty of iodine is introduced via fish foods and water changes. Direct supplementation may even be a bit hazardous, since iodine is difficult to test (due to its many different forms) and is toxic at just above normal levels. Therefore, water exchange should be the first action to counter persistently low iodine levels. In closed systems where the biological uptake of iodine is unusually high (e.g. kelp bed biotope aquaria), it may become necessary to directly add supplemental iodine. It is certainly acceptable to use less than the recommended dosage, but otherwise carefully follow the product manufacturer's instructions. Aquarists tend to use either Lugol's solution (which is part iodine and part iodide) or potassium iodide.

Ammonia concentration will be of greatest concern while the aquarium system is becoming established biologically. It should also be checked a few times after increasing feeding, after increasing the bioload (i.e. adding livestock) or after the death of an aquarium animal (particularly if the carcass decomposed to any extent before it was discovered and removed). Be aware that ammonia is typically present in two different forms when dissolved in seawater. In its polar state, it is referred to as free ammonia (NH$_4$). Ammonia is highly toxic in its free form, which can easily pass through membranes and extensively damage tissues. The ionized form, referred to as ammonium (NH$_4^+$), is only a little less toxic than free ammonia. However, because this charged form does not easily move through membranes, it is significantly less dangerous. Thus, ammonia tests that bear results for each form of ammonia are preferable. For tests that give results only as total ammonia nitrogen (or TAN), the concentration of un-ionized ammonia can be estimated by plugging the TAN, pH, salinity and temperature of the system water into a percentage un-ionized ammonia calculator (try http://pentairaes.com/amonia-calculator).

Seawater concentrations of ammonia vary from one place to another. They may also vary locally from season to season. TAN can be less than 0.002 ppm (e.g. in brightly sunlit offshore waters) or as much as 0.7 ppm (e.g. in polluted bays or estuaries). Un-ionized ammonia is lethal at concentrations of 0.09-3.35 ppm (approximately 1.3-50 ppm TAN). That being said, many organisms will begin to experience stress at far lower levels.

After the period of cycling has passed and livestock has been introduced to the system, ammonia should always be at undetectably low levels. One should cease all feeding and take action if TAN exceeds 0.1 ppm; concentrations above 0.25 ppm should be considered to be an emergency and attended to immediately. Aquarium products containing binders that instantly neutralize ammonia are widely available and should always be on hand for emergency situations. Large water changes can likewise provide some immediate relief.

Sensitive species such as *Hippocampus abdominalis* cannot withstand even moderate exposure to ammonia for long. Dr. Chris Woods.

As nitrification begins to take place, ammonia will decrease in concentration (ideally to undetectably low levels) as it is converted to nitrite. Though not quite as toxic as ammonia, nitrite can cause serious harm to animals exposed to concentrations above 5.0 ppm. Long-term exposure to levels of 0.2-0.5 ppm is harmful to both fish and invertebrates. More sensitive species can succumb to poisoning at levels as low as 0.1 ppm. Fish that are suffering from nitrite poisoning will appear to have trouble breathing. Cnidarians might close up and expel their stomachs through their mouths. Whenever high nitrite levels require urgent attention, large water changes and/or the above mentioned binders can be utilized. With the onset of the nitrogen cycle, nitrites will eventually drop to undetectable levels as they are increasingly converted into nitrate. Nitrate is relatively nontoxic. Some fishes can tolerate brief exposure to concentrations as high as 550 ppm. Still, in a poorly-kept closed system, nitrate build-up can cause considerable harm to the inhabitants. Nitrate concentrations should not be allowed to exceed 20 ppm; levels below 10 ppm are much safer. Chronic nitrate toxicity is generally exhibited as lethargy, weakened feeding response, loss of color or a poor immune system. Cell development is severely stunted at levels as low as 30 ppm in fishes and invertebrates. Excessive nitrate concentrations also

Heavily planted systems may benefit from iron supplementation. NOAA.

Supplemental O_2 is only necessary in cases of extraordinarily high stocking densities (e.g. aquaculture). Kenneth Wingerter.

tend to promote the growth of nuisance algae. A single, short spike in nitrate can trigger algal blooms that seem to last long after lower nitrate concentrations are reestablished. Large water changes are the simplest and surest remedy for excessive nitrate. Even so, carbon dosing, algal scrubbers and denitrifying filters can be used effectively to curb nitrate (as well as phosphate) levels between water changes.

Phosphorus is found in seawater as particulate phosphorus, inorganic phosphate and dissolved organic phosphate. All marine organisms require phosphate to survive. It is, however, required only in small quantities. This is fortunate because there is typically not very much of it in the natural environment. It is among the most limiting nutrients of temperate flora. Bacteria dominate microalgae in low-phosphate conditions, as they are more effective at scavenging it; however, they eventually lose out to the algae under high-phosphate conditions due to carbon limitation. On average, the phosphate content of natural sweater is around 0.01 ppm. Marine aquarists are sometimes instructed to maintain a low phosphate concentration (from 0.01 down to undetectable levels) as to control undesirable algal growth. Phosphate is usually introduced into the aquarium through feeding (especially overfeeding). It tends to accumulate in closed systems (especially where mechanical filtrants are not cleaned frequently). It is rapidly recycled through the breakdown of solid animal wastes, which may be abundant in aquaria. Excess phosphate does not appear to be very toxic, as concentrations often reach a few ppm in fish-only systems with seemingly no ill effect to the inhabitants. Controlled phosphate spikes might even be advantageous (e.g for seaweed cultivation) when replicating the seasonal fluctuation of dissolved nutrient levels in some ecosystems.

Most marine silica comes from eroded terrestrial sources via river run-off; much of this is ultimately stored on the ocean bottom in the frustules (shell-like structures) of diatoms, forming a fine sediment known as diatomaceous earth. This flow of silica from terrestrial watersheds to marine sediment pretty much runs in a one-way direction. There is, however, some release of silica from anoxic sediments. Silica is found in seawater mainly as silicate (SiO_4). Silicate concentration in natural seawater can reach 1.0 or even 8.0 ppm, but it also can be much lower as stores are exhausted during spring diatom blooms. A concentration of around 0.06 ppm seems to be limiting for diatoms. Elevated silicate concentrations are often blamed for unsightly diatom plagues in marine aquarium systems. Though they are generally not very harmful, silicates do in fact tend to accumulate in closed systems. Controlling silicate levels involves removal through (1) purification of the mixing/top-off water, (2) use of silicate-free aquarium salts and additives, (3) moderate feeding, (4) frequent water changes and (5) the use of certain chemical filtrants. A concentration of around 1.0 ppm is acceptable and will be sufficient for certain sponges and mollusks to construct their spicules and shells.

Iron is required in some quantity by all organisms and has been shown to be limiting in temperate and polar seas. Much of this heavy metal is carried to the ocean by dust storms. Dissolved forms of iron may be released from deposits of ferric iron (i.e. rust) in anoxic sediments. A concentration of around 0.01 ppm is usually adequate, though it may need to be replenished often in systems that have an abundance of macroalgae.

Cyanobacteria were the first oxygen-producing (or oxygenic) organisms when they appeared around 2.8 billion years ago, a time when the Earth's atmosphere was very nearly anoxic. Today, oxygen accounts for some 21% of atmospheric gases, nearly all of which is generated via photosynthesis. This gas (O_2) is fairly soluble in seawater, particularly at cold temperatures. Due to vigorous mixing, shallow waters in the higher latitudes are generally well oxygenated. Consequently, few intertidal and even fewer subtidal animals there are adapted to oxygen-depleted conditions. It is therefore important to always maintain oxygen concentrations in aquaria at a saturated level. Being as the solubility of oxygen decreases with increasing temperature, warmer waters can hold less dissolved oxygen than cooler waters. At sea level (one atmosphere of pressure), 35‰ salinity and 12.8°C (55°F), for example, water that is fully air-saturated can

As they tend to be fed rather generously, temperate aquaria require aggressive water quality control. Kenneth Wingerter.

hold as much as 8.51 ppm dissolved oxygen (DO). If the temperature of these waters is raised to room temperature (21°C (70°F)), this would drop to around 7.25 ppm. So, when the aquarium water temperature is within an acceptable range (that is, cool), DO levels will probably be more than sufficient to meet the respiratory needs of the livestock. But again, coldwater marine plants and animals are poorly adapted to withstand even minor hypoxia. Making matters worse, the rising temperature correspondingly increases an organism's metabolism (i.e. its oxygen demand). Consequently, an overheated, oxygen-starved coldwater marine aquarium (especially one that is dirty or overstocked) can crash very quickly. Most often, when proper water temperatures are maintained, it is unnecessary to add supplemental oxygen to a properly equipped coldwater aquarium. So long as the water is well-circulated throughout the system, gas exchange that takes place at the water surface, in the trickle filter, skimmer, etc. will be sufficient to maintain saturated DO levels.

The word "redox" is an acronym that comes from "reduction" and "oxidation." Oxidation is the loss of electrons from a substance while reduction is a gain (i.e. each additional electron a molecule acquires reduces its electrical charge). Reduction and oxidation always occur simultaneously, as there must be a receiver for the donation to take place. Reducing and oxidizing capacity (or redox potential) is a good indicator of overall aquarium water quality. Redox potential is measured in millivolts. Redox potential should (around normal marine aquarium pH values) be approximately 350 mV. Redox levels drop steadily as contaminants (particularly dissolved organics) accumulate; they tend to be lowest right after feeding time. Redox levels can be stabilized with the tightly controlled use of ozone.

Aquarists have a wide array of water testing methods and technologies to choose from. Older aquarists are probably most familiar with tests that involve titrations or evaluating color charts. More and more electronic options are becoming available. These devices utilize special probes that are capable of obtaining very precise results. Readings are clearly shown on a digital display. Some electronic water testers are small, portable, hand-held instruments (known as pens), whereas others are designed for more continuous use. The latter types are often consolidated into some kind of master monitor. Often, these monitors additionally function as controllers. Various control features allow the user to tightly schedule the operation of some pieces of equipment (lighting, wavemakers, etc.) or program other pieces of equipment (chillers, dosers, etc.) to automatically respond to changes in water parameters. For example, surface fans can be programmed to operate only while the system water is above some preset maximum temperature. Controllers/monitors also serve as alarm systems, as most units are capable of contacting the user in the event of an emergency. Video monitors can be installed and used remotely as an additional safeguard.

2. Water Changes and Cleaning

The marine environment (with the exception of the intertidal zone) is generally quite stable, with changes of chemistry or temperature occurring slowly, if at all. It is also (except in upwelling zones) relatively nutrient-poor and low in DOM. This is in sharp contrast with many closed aquarium systems, where biologically essential substances are eventually depleted while toxic waste products continue to accumulate. Consequently, all closed systems (even massive ones with cutting edge life support systems) benefit from regular water changes. Since most synthetic seawater formulations closely resemble the composition of natural seawater, water exchange helps to restore the chemical environment to an overall optimal state.

Water change regimens vary with respect to size and frequency. In order to maintain a stable chemical environment, smaller but frequent exchange is preferable to that which is infrequent but large. Smaller aquarium systems tend to require higher rates of exchange. A weekly water change of around 20% should be sufficient for a well-equipped and moderately stocked aquarium system. Under normal circumstances, no more than 25% of the total system volume should need to be changed at once. As a matter of fact, exchanging too much water at one time can shock the living inhabitants; 50% works as a good place to set a daily maximum. For instance, if major parameters do not return to within acceptable levels after the first 50% exchange, then you should perform another water change (up to 50%) on the following day, and maybe another the next day and so on, until conditions are acceptable and stable.

Good tank cleaning practices can improve water clarity and significantly reduce the need for aggressive water exchange. The tank cleaning "gets done" frequently if it is simple and painless—a gain for the appearance of the aquarium and the health of its inhabitants. The mechanical filter medium, for example, will get serviced more often if it is in clear view and is easy to reach. Doing any kind of manual work in a tankful of chilly water can get uncomfortable. An aquarist can stay a little warmer and drier with just a couple of cheap service items. With some good aquarium tongs or grabbers, one may not often need to reach into the water at all. Those that might need to reach into cold waters for extended periods of time will appreciate a pair of heavy-duty, waterproof, aquarium-safe, full-arm length gloves (e.g. Aqua Gloves).

Most manual aquarium cleaning involves wiping the tank panels. When cleaning the aquarium walls, be sure to use only scrubber pads or blades that are specially made for your type of tank construction. Blue-colored implements are usually made only for glass and hard plastics while white implements (which are softer and less prone to scratching) are suitable for acrylic and other soft plastics. Some types of scrapers allow aquarists to keep their hands warm and dry during use. For small aquaria, the classic pad on a stick will do the job just fine. For larger (and especially deeper) aquaria, scrapers that attach magnetically through the panel to the handle are preferable. Be aware that any tiny piece of hard grit that gets under a pad or blade can scratch a tank made of any material including glass. For this reason, it is best when wiping panels to work from the top of the tank to the bottom with clean tools.

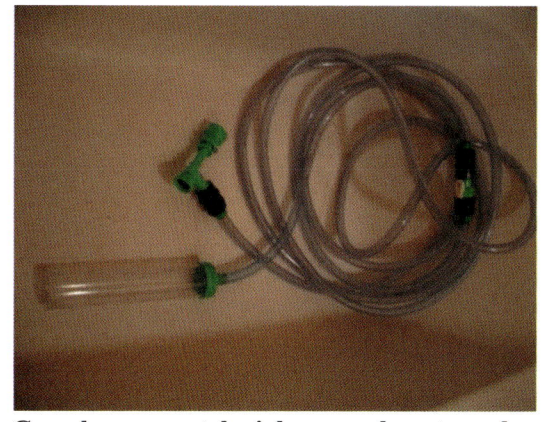

Gravel vacuum-style siphons can be extremely handy for working on small tanks. Kenneth Wingerter.

Many find that the job is done most quickly and with the least scratching by using a pad from the top to just above the substrate whilst surfaces below this point are carefully attended to with a scraper. When finished, thoroughly rinse all cleaning tools under tap water before returning them to storage. Bottom siphoning is usually performed while draining the tank during a water change. It is best done after the panels have been wiped and the resulting particulates have been allowed to settle out. A long section of vinyl tubing can be used for this purpose. Sometimes, a long wand may be used at the business end of the hose to serve as a handle for probing into deeper crevasses within the rockwork. The tubing diameter can expand broadly at the bottom to form a "gravel vacuum" wherein the flow is just sufficient to tumble and stir the substrate but not draw it up and away with the waste water. Some such wands are fitted with a strainer to prevent animals from getting sucked up through the opening. An easy way to start the siphon (without using your mouth, which is rather unsanitary) is to (1) submerge and fill the entire hose under the water in the tank, (2) plug one of the hose ends with your thumb, and (3) carefully pull the plugged end of the hose from the tank and into a receptacle (bucket, sink, etc.) before (4) releasing your thumb from the end to initiate flow. The incurrent end must be at a higher level than the excurrent end for the siphon to start. It may help to use a clamp to keep the submerged end of the hose firmly in place.

When performing aquarium maintenance in a nicely carpeted or furnished area, it is always a good idea to use a highly absorbent drop cloth or mat to protect rugs, flooring, etc. It is likewise smart to have an empty trash bucket and a few big, dry towels at hand.

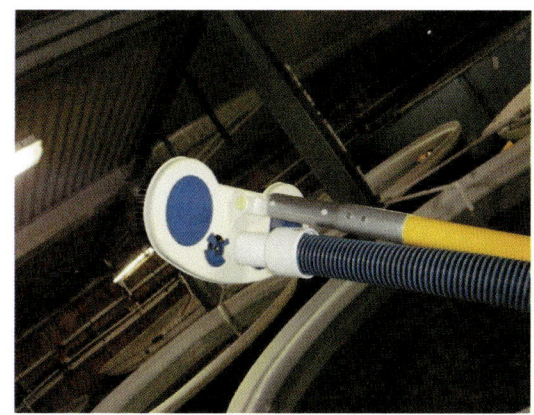

For larger tasks, something a bit burlier will be required. Kenneth Wingerter.

VI. Aquarium Species

1. Natural History

Average surface water temperatures of the equatorial region have probably not exceeded 33°C (91°F) since the late Permian Period (255-248 mya). The upper heat tolerance of modern equatorial marine lifeforms is around 35°C (95°F), indicating adaptation to a thermally stable environment. Ancient mid-latitude mangrove forests died back and were replaced by salt marshes after a period of cooling (followed by mass extinctions) in the late Cretaceous Period (75-66 mya). It was during this time that most living forms of marine flora and fauna emerged. The early Tertiary Period (65-24 mya) marked the beginning of yet another episode of even more dramatic global cooling. Prior to this, differences of temperature between the equator and the poles were probably no more than 5 degrees C (9 degrees F). Surface water temperatures in the North Pacific were still around 18°C (64°F) by the Eocene Epoch (54 mya). By the middle of the Miocene Epoch (14 mya), glaciers had already completely blanketed the once ice-free continent of Antarctica. Ice sheets then began to cover the northern land masses as well as the Arctic Ocean by the start of the Pleistocene Epoch (2 mya). Pleistocene glaciation appears to have further driven the temperature gradients that characterize the tropical, temperate and polar regions, establishing present-day latitudinal changes in species distribution.

Most coldwater marine species are derived from tropical and warm-temperate ancestors. During the first cool period of the Cenozoic Era (late Eocene or early Oligocene Epoch (35-30 mya)), a few coldwater species (e.g. cockles and razor clams) emerged in the Northeast Pacific Ocean and spread westward. Familiar temperate rocky shore communities first appeared in the late Oligocene Epoch. A brief global warming event in the early middle Miocene Epoch initiated the expansion of tropical and subtropical climate belts, facilitating (1) the poleward spread of warm-water species and (2) the westward spread of Northeast Pacific species. Many more species emerged in the middle of the late Miocene in the Northeast Pacific region (with the appearance of large kelps) before spreading westward. Whether a coldwater species originated in the Northeast or Northwest Pacific Ocean, cold adaptation seems to have occurred primarily in the Northeast region. In other words, North Pacific coldwater-adapted biota overwhelmingly first appeared on the American side (from warm-water ancestors) and eventually disbursed to the west. Though the primary direction of invasion during the early Miocene Epoch was westward, a reversal occurred during the late Miocene Epoch, leading to a homogenization of the North Pacific biota.

Coldwater species arose a bit earlier in the North Atlantic Ocean (many archaic cold-adapted soft-bottom forms can still be found on both sides). The North Atlantic Ocean was separated from the North Pacific Ocean until the late Miocene (5 mya) with the opening of the Bering Strait. This northern opening allowed for the exchange of biota between the North Pacific and the North Atlantic oceans. By and large, this was an invasion of North Atlantic waters by Pacific forms. These transarctic invaders included various red algae and kelps, eelgrass (*Zostera* spp.), sea urchins (*Strongylocentrotus* spp.), periwinkles (*Littorina* spp.), auks and soft-shelled clams. By around 3.5 mya, North Atlantic and arctic Pliocene biotas had changed dramatically. The intensity of the eastward invasion was so great that a wave of extinction fell over the whole North Atlantic region, with the American side enduring the greatest loss. Many North Atlantic red algae and kelp, barnacles, sea stars and sea urchins are derived from North Pacific ancestors. As many as 83% of the mollusks and half of all soft-bottom fauna in the Northwest Atlantic Ocean are descended from Northeast Pacific species. Perhaps 70% of late Pliocene Epoch species from both the eastern and western North Pacific Ocean still survive. No major extinctions are thought to have taken place in the North Pacific Ocean since the Eocene Epoch, though some warm-water taxa underwent minor extinctions during the Pliocene and early Pleistocene Epochs.

Temperature is a strong factor in both the latitudinal and depth distribution of all marinelife. For example, the sea star *Asterias forbesi* has a fairly wide depth range off of the Virginian coast, but is restricted to shallows above the thermocline where it occurs further north in the Gulf of Maine. Similarly, coastal fishes of Puget Sound, Washington may be found in a similar temperature layer (or isotherm) in Monterey Bay, California, though at a much greater depth. The maximum temperature at which a species can survive establishes an equatorward summer boundary, while the maximum temperature at which a species can repopulate an area through recruitment establishes an equatorward winter boundary. The minimum temperature at which a species can survive establishes a poleward winter boundary, while the minimum temperature at which a species can recruit establishes a poleward summer boundary. There are sometimes a number of discreet populations within a species that are specially adapted to the climate of a particular geographic region. Several physiological races of the mummichog (*Fundulus heteroclitus*), for example, are distributed along a wide stretch of the U.S. East Coast.

Geographic boundaries of marine species are set primarily by thermal tolerance. These boundaries can be quite sharp where there are points of extreme temperature change (e.g. Point Conception, California and Cape Hatteras, North Carolina). Seasonal change is a bit more pronounced in the North Atlantic Ocean due to the strong influence of continental weather fronts. Maximum summer temperatures are higher in North Atlantic surface waters than in the North Pacific region. Water temperatures may range from 6.7°C to 30.6°C (44°F to 87°F) along the coast of Virginia, whereas the Bay Area of California has an annual range of less than 5 degrees C (8 degrees F). There is a much less abrupt boundary between cold-temperate and warm-temperate regions of the U.S. West Coast than there is on the East Asian coast. The barrier between warmer and cooler water masses is quite sharp along the islands of Japan. Along the North American Pacific Coast, on the other hand, there is an area of thermal transition that extends for over 1,000 kilometers (621 miles). These very different temperature gradients are thought to be a major cause of the asymmetrical origin of cold-adapted species across the North Pacific Ocean.

The warm and nutrient-poor waters of the tropics have acted as a strong barrier to the exchange of coldwater species between the northern and southern temperate regions. We see this clearly among the macroalgae. Particularly for a brown alga, the giant kelp (*Macrocystis pyrifera*) is exceptional in having populations on both sides of the equator. A few red and green algae (*Gracilaria confervoides*, *Ulva lactuca*, etc.) are both tropical and temperate (i.e. cosmopolitan) in distribution. But while *Laminaria* spp. are numerous and widespread across northern temperate seas, they are represented by only a few species with restricted distributions in the south. The entire genus *Fucus* is confined to the north; Australia and New Zealand have their own endemic fucoid genera (*Acrocarpia*, *Hormosira*, etc.).

***Fundulus heteroclitus* occurs from 28-52° N and can survive at water temperatures ranging from 10-24°C (50-75°F). NOAA.**

High latitude stony coral reefs can exist (albeit with a modest coral diversity) where oceanic currents bring warm waters and larval recruits. The ecological limits of both tropical and temperate species are represented in these transitional areas. Extending beyond 31° S, the Lord Howe Island Group is home to the most southerly coral reef on Earth. There is an interesting mix of tropical and temperate species there (13 of which are endemic). Though 60% of the 490 fish species reported there are tropical, quite a few subtropical and temperate species are known there as well (e.g. *Amphiprion latezonatus*, *Chaetodontoplus conspicillatus*). In the nearby Solitary Islands, 20% of the 280 fish species reported there are temperate.

Due to differences in oceanic surface current patterns, there is a greater richness of coldwater species on North America's west coast than on its east coast. The northward flowing Gulf Stream of the Northwest Atlantic Ocean delivers fairly warm, subtropical water all of the way up the North Carolinian coast; its surface waters are characteristically temperate only after reaching Cape Hatteras. In contrast, the cold, eastward flowing North Pacific Current runs right into the California Coast at Point Conception, splitting to deliver chilled waters both northward towards Oregon and southward towards Baja California (tropical species are rarely encountered north of Cape San Lucas). We may be seeing a shift in the latitudinal range of some species as a consequence of Holocene (that is, present day) global warming. Already there is evidence on both North American coasts of a general decline in the abundance of coldwater species with a corresponding increase in the abundance of warm-water species.

Though *Anthothoe* spp. is ubiquitous across the temperate Southern Hemisphere, it is totally absent in the north. Graham Bould.

On a global scale, there is a recognizable latitudinal gradient in species richness, with the highest levels of diversity in the tropics and lowest levels in the polar regions. Both biotic and abiotic theories have been proposed to explain this pattern. Abiotic theories include (1) ecological time theory and (2) productivity theory. Ecological time theory asserts that temperate marine biological communities are less diverse than tropical counterparts because they are younger. According to this theory, temperate species have not yet had enough time to adapt to occupy many vacant niches. Perhaps complimentary to this view is productivity theory (or the species-energy hypothesis), which asserts that longer growing seasons in the tropics result in (1) overall higher annual rates of primary production and (2) a greater ability of competing species to partition resources (both spatially and temporally), thereby promoting higher levels of species coexistence. Biotic theories include (1) competition theory, (2) predation theory and (3) evolutionary speed theory. Competition theory asserts that in the warm, stable tropics, species tend to compete more intensely for space and so are *K*-selected, whereas in the thermally unstable temperate regions, species tend to be limited by physical extremes and so are *r*-selected, with a small handful of hardy species occurring in huge numbers (e.g. *Mytilus* spp.). Predation theory asserts that because there is a generally greater number of predators and parasites in tropical regions, populations of prey species are kept low enough to allow for greater species coexistence, which in turn promotes higher numbers of more specialized predator species. For example, many tropical predatory starfish are specialized to prey on a single species, whereas the temperate starfish *Pisaster ochraceous* may eat two barnacle and six mollusk species (and even accept without hesitation any small animal carcass that it can wrap its arms around). Evolutionary speed theory asserts that overall higher energy levels in the tropics promotes (1) faster life cycles, (2) higher occurrences of mutation and (3) an accelerated natural selection of favorable mutations.

Evolutionary biologists use phylogeny to describe the family history of all life on Earth. Most of us are familiar with the basic taxonomic "tree of life" wherein all known species are organized into groups on the basis of lineage. We are familiar also with systematics, which classifies lifeforms in terms of degrees of relation and gives a unique name to each species. The most prevalent means of naming and classifying species uses a five-kingdom hierarchical scheme. Kingdoms classify organisms at the most basic level. They are followed (in terms of increasing levels of classification) by phylum, class, order, family, genus and then species. Divisions can be identified within some of the groups (subclass, subfamily, etc.). The binomial genus and species designation of an organism is known as its scientific (or "Latin") name. The name of the genus is referred to as the generic epithet and the name of the species as the specific epithet. The generic epithet is always capitalized whereas the specific epithet is never capitalized. When a Latin name is repeated often in text, the generic epithet may be abbreviated. As such, the ruby seadragon (*Phyllopteryx dewysea*) belongs to Kingdom Animalia, Phylum Chordata, Order Actinopterygii, Family Syngnathidae, Subfamily Syngnathinae, Genus *Phyllopteryx* and the species *P. dewysea*. *Phyllopteryx* sp. would be used if identification at the species level is uncertain; *Phyllopteryx* spp. would be used to denote all members of the genus.

2. The Microbes

As a group, the microbes can be best described as relatively simple organisms that are so miniscule they can be seen clearly by the human eye only with the aid of a microscope. The group is comprised of prokaryotes (bacteria and archaea), protozoans and a few of the tiniest animals. The bacteria and archaea are characteristically single-celled organisms (ranging in size from 0.2-2.0 micrometers in diameter) that lack membrane-bound nuclei and organelles. They are ubiquitous and are incredibly diverse. The archaea (sometimes referred to as archaebacteria) form a much smaller (though more ancient) group. The prokaryotes are adapted to live in nearly every corner of the Earth. Spirochaetes occupy the sediment on the deepest seafloor. Methanogenic bacteria and many archaea can be found in anoxic sediments. Psychrophiles can be found in permanently cold areas and are capable of withstanding freezing temperatures. Halophilic bacteria live in areas of extremely highly salinity. Thermoacidophilic bacteria live in hot, acidic (e.g. hot springs) environments. Green sulfur bacteria are among the most efficient photoautotrophs, capable of carrying out photosynthesis at 260 feet (80 meters) depth while consuming sulfuric substances from decaying organic matter and hydrothermal vents.

Most prokaryotic phytoplankton belong to the cyanobacteria. At only 0.5-1.0 micrometers, cyanobacteria are the smallest members of the phytoplankton in terms of physical size (they may however clump together, forming much larger balls or chains). They are most common in tropical seas. The smallest cyanobacteria species occur in the tropics, while the largest occur in temperate regions. Cyanobacteria contain the phycobilin pigment phycocyanin, which enhances absorption of light into the orange and blue-green parts of the light spectrum.

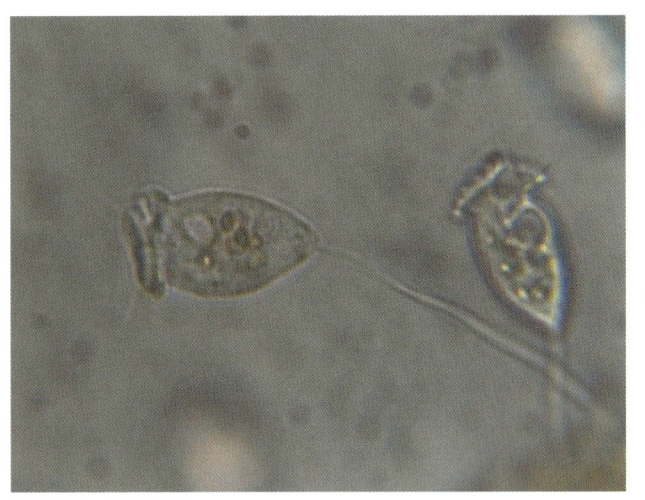

Many "pure" starter cultures actually contain a variety of contaminants such as *Vorticella*. Kenneth Wingerter.

Aerobic heterotrophic bacteria (such as *Bacterium* spp.) take up amino acids that are released from decomposing organic matter to produce NH_4^+/NH_3. These nitrogenous waste products are subsequently oxidized (as they are used as a source of energy) by those aerobic, chemoautotrophic microbes known as the nitrifying bacteria. *Nitrosomonas* and their relatives convert ammonia and ammonium into nitrite, which is converted into nitrate by *Nitrobacter* and their relatives. In so doing, these microbes detoxify some of the most poisonous and rapidly accumulating metabolites that build up in aquaria. Without them, recirculating aquarium systems would be nearly impossible to maintain.

For coldwater aquarists in particular, patience is required during the cycling period. Typical coldwater marine aquarium temperatures are significantly lower than those corresponding to the optimal metabolic (and therefore reproductive) rates of these microbes. For this reason, while a tropical aquarist can expect the full or near-full development of the nitrifying microbial community within a couple of weeks, a coldwater aquarist might have to wait several weeks or even months for the same result.

Anaerobic denitrifying bacteria may be inhibited even by a modest presence of oxygen (which is toxic to many of them) and can thusly be categorized on the basis of oxygen tolerance. They are most numerous in deeper pore waters of the substratum, where DO levels are minimal due to the respiration of aerobic organisms in the above layers. Strict anaerobes only tolerate dissolved oxygen concentrations of ≤ 0.4% saturation and moderate anaerobes tolerate concentrations of 0.8-2.5% while aerotolerant anaerobes tolerate concentrations of ≥2.5%. Microaerophilic bacteria survive at lower oxygen levels but nevertheless prefer anaerobic conditions (or those with >10% carbon dioxide). Facultative anaerobic bacteria can survive in (and indeed benefit from) the presence oxygen, but are capable of switching to an anaerobic mode of respiration when oxygen is lacking. The denitrifying bacteria genera *Bacillus*, *Denitrobacillas*, *Thiobacillus*, *Micrococcus*, *Pseudomonas* and others can occur in marine aquaria. These microbes convert nitrate into nitrogen gas. They populate the deeper layers of the substrate, within the core of porous stone or in an anoxic biological filter medium. Sulfate reducing bacteria (Phylum Thiopneutes) can be found in denitrifying filters that are fed a sulfur-based compound (e.g. sodium thiosulfate).

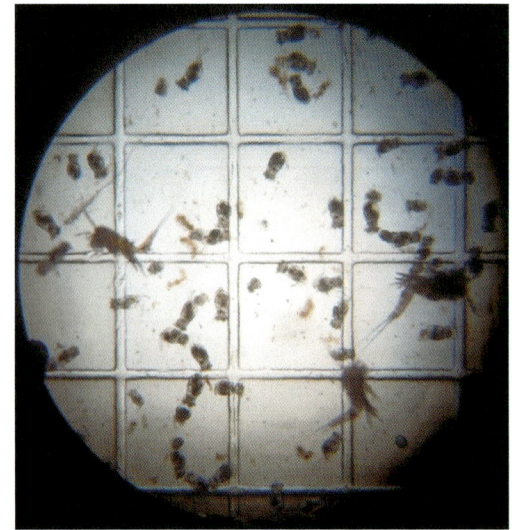

Microfood organisms such as rotifers and copepods have gained importance in the aquarium industry. Kenneth Wingerter.

Many microorganisms feed heavily upon bacteria. The ciliates may be the most ubiquitous and important of bacterivores. Where bacterial densities are high, an individual ciliate may capture as many as 10,000-50,000 cells per hour. Among the largest of single-celled organisms, most ciliates range from 10-100 micrometers in length (with some being as small a couple of micrometers and others as large as a few millimeters). Some ciliates have a protective, proteinaceous barrel- or vase-shaped covering called a lorica (those that lack this covering are referred to as naked). A few loricate ciliates (e.g. the tintinnid ciliates) are abundant and ecologically quite important.

Flagellates are similarly important protozoans. They are usually about 2-100 micrometers long excluding the flagellum. Like cilia, flagella are used primarily for locomotion and feeding. Although a single flagellate can consume only 4-200 bacterial cells per hour, they are considered to be major bacterivores due to their typically high population densities; it is not uncommon for flagellates to occur in densities of up to 10 million individuals per liter. Many of these adaptable organisms are capable of mixotrophy. The flagellates are a very diverse, distantly related functional group rather than a discreet taxonomic group with closely shared ancestry; the dinoflagellates are related to certain phytoplankton, while the choanoflagellates are related to the sponges. Certain photosynthetic dinoflagellates (i.e. zooxanthellae) are endosymbiotic with many shallow water sea anemones (e.g. *Anemonia sulcata*, *Anthopleura elegantissima*).

Concentrated algal pastes can be conveniently used to feed microfood cultures. Kenneth Wingerter.

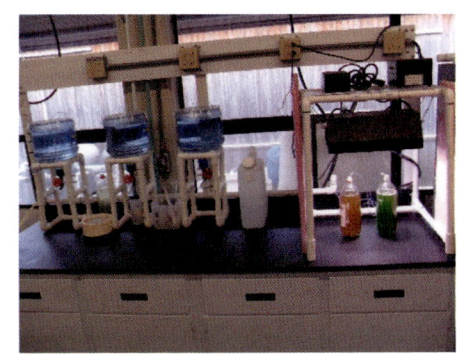

Yet another important group of marine protozoa are the amoebas. Marine amoebas tend to bear a calcareous protective shell. Two such amoeboid groups, the foraminiferans and the radiolarians, are responsible for sediments formed from their discarded shells called oozes. Foraminiferans have extensions called pseudopodia that reach out into the water column to snatch bacteria and phytoplankton. Certain larger "forams" harbor gardens of symbiotic dinoflagellates. Generally, foraminiferans occur at densities of no more than 100 per liter. Radiolarians are roughly similar to foraminiferans, but usually have siliceous shells and are considerably less abundant, being found at densities of around just 20 per liter.

Despite their complexity, many rotifers are actually smaller than some common unicellular organisms. While the rotifers claim over 1,800 species and their own phylum, they are poorly represented in the marine environment. They range in size from 40 micrometers to 3 millimeters long, but most are 100-500 micrometers in length. Many are capable of switching between a benthic and pelagic existence in order to maximally exploit phytoplankton and POM food sources. Some species are encased in a tough, fibrous lorica. A ciliated crown (or corona) sits atop the center of the head. The mouth is located within the midventral side of the

Being clean and orderly can help to prevent the contamination of microfood cultures. Kenneth Wingerter.

corona. The trunk may be either elongated or saccular. The foot is narrow and holds one to four toes. Though they are scarce in the sea, certain brackish/marine rotifer species (e.g. *Brachionus plicatilis*) have taken on great commercial value in aquaculture as a feed for larval fishes and crustaceans.

A newly set up marine aquarium is pretty much a barren, sterile environment. A healthy microbial community can be established by "seeding" the system with a combination of beneficial microorganisms. Traditionally, aquarists have seeded their tanks with a handful of "live" sand from a beach or an established aquarium. As of late, aquaria can be seeded using various inoculants. A great variety of bacteria and protozoa can be obtained as such through aquacultural and scientific supply companies. Aquarium inoculants are most often available as bottled liquids, though some freeze-dried powders can be found. The use of these products may be preferable to the older, less discriminate method of substrate transfer in that it carries no risk of introducing nuisance or disease organisms (benthic diatoms, fish parasites, etc.). Strains of bacteria and archaea that are adapted to cooler waters are strongly preferred as they will generally reduce cycling time and form more stable cultures in coldwater aquaria.

3. The Flora

There are at least 10,000 primary producer species in the marine biome. The great majority of these are photoautotrophs. Marine autotrophs are considered to be either benthic or planktonic in habit. Two sargassum weed species live an entirely planktonic existence, where many small fishes and invertebrates live among their fronds. But with few exceptions, the macroalgae are restricted to shallow, hard sea bottoms.

Some use the term plant to refer to any photosynthetic organism, specifically referring to members of Kingdom Plantae as "true" plants. It is important to recognize, however, that most formal systems classify algae as protozoa and all cyanobacteria (the so-called blue-green algae) as prokaryotes. The term flora usually refers to the larger, more complex true plants and plant-like algae. In a five-kingdom phylogenetic scheme, single-celled algae are sometimes classified with the protozoa (Protista) while multicellular algae are classified as plants (Plantae). The term algae is itself a blanket term, as it describes a very broad group of only distantly related organisms. These are divided on the basis of photopigment content into the brown (Phaeophyta), red (Rhodophyta) and green (Chlorophyta) algae.

There are about 1,500 species of brown algae. They are almost entirely marine and are primarily represented in the temperate regions. Of all the brown seaweeds, the leafy kelps are certainly of the most interest to aquarists. Kelps can grow incredibly fast and reach huge sizes. Bull kelp can grow to 60 meters (200 feet) from a spore in a matter of months. Kelps do, however, have a tendency for seasonal growth patterns, and might die back significantly at certain times of the year. Their cell walls produce a layer of mucilage that is composed of algin or alginic acid. Some brown algae can developed a fairly complex internal structure, and may even have plant-like vascular tissues (known as sieve tubes). The brown algae produce chlorophyll a, chlorophyll c and a handful of carotenoids. It is the carotenoid fucoxanthin that imparts the rich golden brown hue to this group. Important temperate phaeophyte genera include *Laminaria*, *Macrocystis*, *Nereocystis*, *Postelsia*, *Pelvetia*, *Alaria*, *Egregia*, *Agarum*, *Punctaria*, *Chordaria*, *Sargassum*, *Cutleria*, *Fucus* and *Ectocarpus*.

There are about 4,000 species of red algae. These too are primarily marine, but are most abundant in the tropics. There is nevertheless a nice variety of red algae from the midlatitudes, which arguably includes some of the most impressive ornamental seaweeds. The diversity and abundance of large, fleshy red macroalgae is highest in cold-temperate regions whereas those in the tropics tend be small, simple, filamentous forms. Red macroalgae are usually found growing attached to stones or other algae, though free-living forms exist. Their cell walls contain a gelatin-based layer of mucilage. Some (e.g. the coralline algae) form a calcium carbonate crust. Owing to a few light harvesting adaptations, they are often capable of growing at greater depths where there is less competition for space with other macroalgae (some species have been recorded at depths as great as 200 meters (656 feet)). In addition to chlorophyll *a* and some carotenoid pigments, red algae contain the phycobilin pigment phycoerythrin. It is mainly these and the carotenoids that are responsible for the ruddy hue of this group. Important temperate rhodophyte genera include *Porphyra*, *Smithora*, *Nemalion*, *Gelidium*, *Lithophyllum*, *Corallina*, *Gracilaria*, *Gigartina*, *Hypoglossum*, *Iridaea*, *Palmaria*, *Dasya* and *Chondrus*.

There are about 7,000 species of green algae. They are regarded as the most diverse algal group, ranging from simple unicellular to complex multicellular forms (e.g. *Caulerpa scalpelliformis*). They are primarily freshwater but can be found in marine (and even terrestrial) environments. They are also believed to be the progenitors of land plants. Though they compete poorly with other algal groups at depth, some hardy green algae are very successful in the physically harsh (though brightly sunlit) shallows. They often have a thick, well-defined cell wall with an outer layer of pectin. The green algae have a pigment complex that is quite similar to that of the flowering plants. Most examples contain the pigments chlorophyll *a* and *b*, xanthophylls and β-carotene. It is the only group that produces chlorophyll *b*. Its characteristic green coloration comes from the chlorophyll pigments. Important temperate chlorophyte genera include *Codium*, *Caulerpa*, *Hormosira*, *Phaeophila*, *Ulva*, *Enteromorpha*, *Monostroma*, *Prasiola*, *Chaetomorpha*, *Bryopsis* and *Acrocarpia*.

True plants have specialized vascular tissues. There are relatively few temperate marine true plants, most of which are seagrasses. Seagrasses are true flowering plants, producing pollen, flowers, fruit and seed. Water currents disperse seeds as far away as 130 kilometers (80 miles), though most usually settle close to the mother plants. Seagrasses also reproduce vegetatively by extension of the rhizome. Thus, a single meadow may be composed of the clones of just a few individuals, which may be as old as a thousand years. The predominantly temperate seagrass genera include *Amphibolis*, *Posidonia*, *Phyllospadix* and *Zostera*. A few representatives of tropical genera such as *Halodule*, *Syringodium* and *Thalassodendron* can be found in (especially southern) temperate coastal habitats. The ranges of two or more seagrass species may broadly overlap; in some cases, different species can even be found growing with one another in intermingled beds. Seagrass meadows are biogenic habitats that provide shelter for a great many types of organisms; 70 species of fish and almost 200 species of invertebrates can be found in the *Zostera* beds of the U.S. Pacific Northwest coast alone. Bacterial films and algae that cover the leaf blades are grazed on by harpacticoid copepods and other tiny invertebrates, which are in turn preyed on heavily by small fishes and larger invertebrates.

4. The Fauna

The term fauna refers to phyla in Kingdom Animalia, though loosely; as we have seen, due to their relative small size and simplicity, some primitive animals can be regarded as microbes. Here, we will include among the fauna only larger, metazoan (or multicellular) organisms. Aquarists tend to divide aquarium fauna into two major groups: fishes and invertebrates. They tend also to categorize invertebrates (which are overwhelmingly benthic in habit) as either mobile or sessile (i.e. sedentary). Most of the mobile epifaunal invertebrates that inhabit temperate coastal habitats are carnivorous, while the majority of sessile epifaunal invertebrates there

Avoiding contamination can be especially challenging when handling multiple species. Kenneth Wingerter.

Live rotifers are an excellent feed for many zooplanktivores, but require a screen of appropriate mesh size. Kenneth Wingerter.

A shockingly wide variety of macroalgae can oftentimes be found growing together in a single area. Gary Houston.

rely on filter feeding to capture POM or plankton that comes in with the tides. The marine filter feeders include a diverse group of invertebrates (barnacles, tube worms, bryozoans, tunicates, corals, bivalve mollusks, sponges, etc.). Some filter feeding invertebrates are capable of sifting through many, many gallons of seawater each day.

There are as many as 5,000 species of marine sponge. The sponges (Phylum Porifera) represent some of the simplest animalian forms. In some respects, their bodies work like a colony of independent cells. There are only a few different cell types, each carrying out a specific function. Sponge morphology, on the other hand, is rather varied. Sponges can occur as little branches or cups as well as massive vases, mounds or encrustations. They may be found in virtually any color, though the brightest forms tend to occur in shallower waters. The shape and hue of an individual species might differ considerably under different environmental conditions. Though they may take on distinct shapes, sponges do not exhibit any true body symmetry. Some can even reassemble themselves after being chopped into pieces.

An outer epithelial layer of flattened cells encases the sponge body like a skin. Beneath this is a gelatinous matrix known as the mesohyl. The rigidity of the body is provided by a skeleton. In most species, the skeleton is made up of a network of tough protein (or spongin), hard little needles (or spicules) or some combination of the two. Spicules are usually either calcium carbonate-based or glasslike. Each species has its own unique form of spicule. A system of canals runs through the animal's skeletal structure. These canals are used to bring food and oxygen into, and waste products out of, the animal. Water enters the canals through tiny holes (or ostia) that cover the animal's body surface. It is then drawn into a chamber that is lined with flagellated collar cells (or choanocytes), so named for the sticky, funnel-shaped collar around the base of each flagellum that is used to catch food particles. From there, the water is pushed out by the activity of the collar cells through larger pores (or oscula). Simple sponges have a single chamber and osculum while larger forms can have multiples of each.

The phylum Porifera is comprised of three classes. Members of the class Hexactinellida, the glass sponges, occur in extremely deep water and are not yet encountered in the aquarium trade. Class Calcarea claims four genera of smaller sponges with limy spicules (all occurring in shallow temperate seascapes), namely *Leucandra*, *Leucilla*, *Leucosolenia* and *Scypha*. Class Demospongiae, which includes all remaining sponges, includes species with glasslike spicules, spongin, and both as well as those with no skeleton at all. Not all types fare well in captivity; Anderson (2001) suggests *Tethya aurantia*, *Polymastia pachymastia*, *Aplysilla glacialis*, *Suberites* sp., *Syringella* spp., *Halichondria* spp., *Cliona* spp. and *Scypha* sp. for aquarium use.

The phylum Cnidaria includes some of the most popular and coveted invertebrate aquarium species. The cnidarians are almost exclusively marine and brackish. Their life cycle involves a benthic polyp stage, a pelagic medusa stage, or both. Polyps can be either solitary or colonial. Their radially symmetric bodies basically consist of a tube or sack. The outer layer of the body wall (or epidermis) is separated from the lining of the digestive cavity (or gastrodermis) by a middle layer of tissue (or mesoglea). There is a single opening, the mouth (or hypostome), which is surrounded by tentacles. Specialized cells called nematocysts are produced in the epidermis and are concentrated over the tentacles. Nematocysts are best described as capsules containing tiny harpoons on long threads that are launched when physical contact is made with another animal. These so-called stinging cells may be deployed for either defense or predation. Each may be discharged only one time, so the animal must continuously replace used stinging cells. By and large, cnidarians are predators. There are some, nonetheless, that feed mainly on POM, phytoplankton and bacterioplankton that they trap in a mucus secreted around the mouth and oral disc. There are others that harbor intracellular symbionts such as zoochlorellae and zooxanthellae.

The phylum Cnidaria is represented by three classes. Class Hydrozoa (which includes the hydras, hydroids, hydramedusae, chondrophorans, siphonophorans and hydrocorallines) is highly diverse. Hydrozoans may be of a polyp or medusa form, or undergo both stages in their development. Class Scyphozoa includes those animals referred to as the jellyfishes. Class Anthozoa, which includes the sea anemones, soft corals and stony corals, is arguably the most important class of invertebrates to marine aquarists. Anthozoans lack a medusa stage. Their bodies are radially partitioned by septa (or mesenteries). With the exception of the sea anemones, anthozoans are primarily colonial and often may reproduce asexually by budding.

Class Anthozoa is divided into several subclasses and orders that are worthy of mention here. Subclass Octocorallia includes the soft corals, sea pens, sea whips and sea fans. In the latter two, skeletal

Sponges such as *Acarnus erithacus* feed on microplankton as well as POM. Chad King.

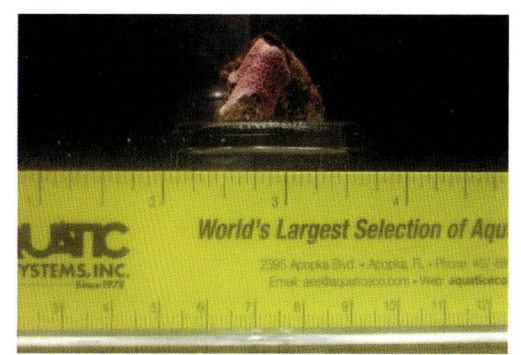

Hydrozoans such as *Stylantheca* require a rich and steady source of microplankton for survival and growth. Kenneth Wingerter.

***Alcyonium* feeds on both phytoplankton and tiny zooplankton. Parent Géry.**

Zoanthids such as *Parazoanthus* differ from sea anemones in that they tend to be colonial whereas the latter are generally solitary. Albert Kok.

The cerianthid diet consists primarily of zooplankton and marine snow. Chad King.

structure is provided internally by a woody or horny substance called gorgonin. The octocorals are characterized as having a set of exactly eight tentacles. Though the sea fans and sea whips are fairly well represented there, only a handful of soft corals (e.g. *Cladiella australis*, *Alcyonium glumeratum*) inhabit cooler coastal waters. Subclass Hexacorallia includes the sea anemones, stony corals and their relatives. Hexacorallia is divided further into the orders Zoantharia, Actiniaria, Antipatharia, Ceriantharia, Scleractinia and Corallimorpharia. The zoanthids are usually small, simple polyps (either solitary or colonial) that lack a skeleton. The actiniarians are almost totally solitary and sessile (though some will readily detach and drift to a new location). The main body (or column) attaches to the substrate by means of an adhesive pedal disc. These animals can dramatically change size by changing their internal hydrostatic pressure to expand or contract. If disturbed, they might expel nematocyst-rich filaments (or acontia) in defense. The black corals and tube-dwelling anemones once made up the subclass Ceriantipatharia. While the two groups do not resemble each other superficially, the similarity of larval ceriantharians to black coral polyps was the rationale for the grouping. Order Ceriantharia includes the cerianthids (or tube anemones). The Cerianthids are anemonelike, but differ from true sea anemones in at least one significant respect; rather than a pedal disc, cerianthids have a tapered foot that is adapted to burrowing into soft sea bottoms. Tentacles are arranged in two whorls. The peripheral feeding tentacles are long and slender while the median labial tentacles are short and stubby. The long, slender column is encased in a tough, pliable tube formed from the discharged threads of specialized nematocycts. More similar to the sea anemones internally is the order Scleractinia. Known as the stony corals, they differ from sea anemones in having the ability to secrete a calcium carbonate skeleton at their base. The physical conformation of the polyp (e.g. the septal pattern) has an effect on the shape of the skeleton. Often, skeletal shape is further determined by factors such as light exposure, orientation to currents, etc. Most scleractinians are colonial. The skeletal structure of an entire colony is referred to as a corallum. Scleractinians are restricted mainly to warm, sunlit waters. The relative few stony corals that occur in cooler waters tend to be solitary and, unlike so many of their tropical cousins, do not harbor zooxanthellae. Members of Order Corallimorpharia are structurally similar to stony corals but lack any kind of skeleton. Corallimorpharians (or mushroom anemones) resemble sea anemones in having a pedal disc; tentacles are, however, greatly reduced. Perhaps aptly dubbed the "coldwater aquarist's *Acropora*," the corallimorpharian genus *Corynactis* is a common feature of temperate reef biotopes.

There are many similarly shaped (though only distantly related) organisms that are referred to as worms (flatworms, peanut worms, ribbon worms, etc.). Few of these phyla carry any importance in the aquarium trade, with the notable exception of the phylum Annelida. Annelida claims approximately 9,000 species in three classes, Hirudinea (the leeches), Oligochaeta (the earthworms and freshwater worms) and Polychaeta (the bristled worms). The typical annelid body is cylindrical, elongate and segmented. A thin, flexible cuticle covers the body wall. Their internal body plan is more complex than the previously described phyla. They have a complete digestive system that extends from the mouth to an anus. They have well-developed musculature that allows for better mobility. Most have advanced circulatory and nervous systems. They may respire directly through the cuticle, though some types have large, specialized gill structures. They often are equipped with highly responsive sensory appendages. Among the annelids, it is the polychaetes that are of the most interest to marine aquarists. Class Polychaeta is divided into the subclasses Errantia and Sedentaria. The errant polychaetes can freely move about while those that are sedentary are confined to a tube or burrow. The errantia (e.g. fire worms) are deposit feeders, scavengers and predators while the sedentaria (e.g. lug worms) are deposit feeders and filter feeders.

Scyphozoans require very specialized husbandry and aquarium systems. Kenneth Wingerter.

The arthropods make up one of the largest and most diverse animal phyla. The nervous and circulatory systems of arthropods resemble that of the annelids. And, like the annelids, arthropods are segmented. Arthropods differ from the annelids in that their segments are dissimilar and are grouped into functional regions (most basically the head, thorax and abdomen). Characteristic to the arthropods is a tough exoskeleton that may be shed and replaced as the animal grows. The exoskeleton is composed of chitin that is secreted by special epidermal cells. Joints are formed in the armor where the chitin is thinner and more pliable.

Undoubtedly, of the many marine arthropods, aquarists are most concerned with the crustaceans. Class Crustacea is huge with over 31,000 (some say over 35,000) described species. It includes the barnacles, isopods, amphipods, crabs, shrimps, lobsters and crayfish. The crustacea consistently have five pairs of appendages on six head segments (one pair of mandibles, two pairs of antennae and two pairs of food-handling mouthparts (or maxillae)). The first two or three pairs of walking legs bear pinchers. They are often covered in bristles that are sensitive to touch. The subclass Decapoda (the crabs, shrimps, lobsters and crayfishes) claims around 8,500 of the known crustacean species. This group

Pandalas danae **prefers protected areas such as** *Zostera* **beds. Kenneth Wingerter.**

is overwhelmingly marine. While some are parasitic and a few are totally pelagic, most adult crustacea are epibenthic. These adaptable creatures can have broad local distributions. For example, the coon-stripe shrimp (*Pandalus danae*) may be found in harbors, seagrass meadows, tide pools or estuaries from the intertidal zone down to over 180 meters (600 feet).

Mollusca is another large, varied phylum. It consists of around 100,000 predominantly marine species. The molluscan body plan consists of a head with a mouth and sensory organs, a foot and a bundle of internal organs (or visceral mass) that is encased by the body wall. Some mollusks have a long, rigid tongue-like structure (or radula) that is used to rasp food items from solid surfaces. In many cases, a calcium carbonate-based shell is secreted from a membranous extension on the body wall (or mantle). The mantle surrounds a cavity that contains the anus, gills and excretory pores.

There are seven classes of mollusk, with at least four being of considerable interest to the aquarist. Class Polyplacophora (the chitons) is characterized by a flattened, ovular body shape and a series of eight hard plates (or valves) over the back. The edge of the mantle (or girdle) surrounds (and sometimes covers) the valves. The foot is large and strong. Chitons cling closely and tightly to rocky surfaces where they feed primarily on small benthic algae. Most living molluscan species belong to Gastropoda. This sizable class includes the snails, limpets, abalones and slugs. Most are marine. The basic gastropod body plan consists of a head with tentacles, eyes and a mouth. Many are protected by a spiral shell that is secreted by the animal. In the case of the slugs, this shell is internal, is vestigial and may be lost at maturity. Some snails have a horny or limy plate on the side of the foot that serves as a protective lid when the animal is hiding within its shell. Class Bivalvia includes molluscs that have a hinged pair of valves. Most of the 15,000 bivalve species are marine. The bivalve shell is entirely lined by the mantle. The mantle has two openings, the incurrent and excurrent siphons, to take in and release water. A head and radula are absent. Gills are used for food collection as well as for respiration. Some anchor themselves to hard surfaces by means of strong threads secreted from a gland on the foot. Many are adapted to an infaunal lifestyle. A few are able to bore into solid wood, shell or stone. Class Cephalopoda (the squids, cuttlefishes, octopods and nautiluses) includes some of the most advanced invertebrates. In the cephalopods, the mantle surrounds the visceral mass and covers the body openings and gills. If disturbed, many cephalopods are capable of spurting ink from a gland in the mantle into the surrounding waters as they flee. Extensions of the foot form several arms (usually eight) that are covered with suckers. The arms surround a beaked mouth. The bite of some species administers a paralyzing toxin. In squids and cuttlefish, the shell is internal and greatly reduced. A shell is entirely absent in the octopods. The siphons and mantle cavity are used for locomotion. The squids and cuttlefishes, which have a pair of finlike bodily extensions, are excellent swimmers. While not as adept at swimming, octopods are more comfortable walking along the bottom with their extremely agile arms.

Macrocheira kaempferi **is only appropriate for large deep-water aquaria. Kenneth Wingerter.**

Feather duster worm *Eudistylia polymorpha* **prefers a diet of microplankton and POM. Chad King.**

Echinodermata is an exclusively marine phylum that includes the sea stars, brittle stars, basket stars, sea urchins, sand dollars and sea cucumbers. The radially symmetric echinoderm body plan is almost always arranged into five unsegmented parts. There is a mouth at one end and an anus at the other end of a distinct body axis (the mouth may be dorsally or ventral situated, depending upon body form). The body is supported by an internal limy skeleton and covered with a skin. The skin is often covered with hard plates or spines. Water moves in and out of the animal through a perforated disk (or sieve plate) that is embedded in its skin. An internal hydraulic vascular system controls numerous tube feet (or podia). The podia are often used for feeding as well as for locomotion. The excretory system is poorly developed, as most wastes easily pass through the water vascular system. Echinoderms are nevertheless highly advanced organisms with very well-developed digestive, nervous and reproductive systems.

Unless their highly specialized needs can be properly met, nudibranchs should be left in the sea. Kenneth Wingerter.

The classes and subclasses of Echinodermata vary considerably in form and habit. Probably, the most recognizable class in the group is Stelleroidea, the sea stars. Subclass Asteroidea includes the common starfishes (e.g. *Asterina* spp.). These are mainly flattened and five-pointed in form. There is a central disk from which each arm (or ray) extends. An eyespot is frequently present on the tip of each arm. Some have numerous modified spines (or pedicellariae) that are used to grasp tiny objects. Many can greatly distend the stomach to envelope and draw in food items. Subclass Ophiuroidea (the brittle stars and basket stars) has a markedly more delicate body form than does its asteroid cousin. The arms of ophiuroids are comparatively slender, are far more flexible and do not meet each other at the base. In the basket stars, the arms are branched extensively. One or two small openings at the base of each arm lead to a chamber (or respiratory pouch). The pouch lining takes up oxygen as the body wall pushes water in and out of the chamber. Class Echinoidea (the sea urchins and sand dollars) lacks distinct rays. The echinoid skeleton (or test) is formed from a radial arrangement of hard, tightly jointed plates. In many cases, movable spines fit over bumps on the surface of the plates. In the sea urchins, five paired rows of podia run longitudinally along the test. A flexible lip surrounds the mouth on the underside of the animal. Food is chewed with a jaw-like skeletal structure known as the Aristotle's lantern. Spines are shorter (though more numerous) and the test more flattened in the sand dollars, which are adapted to a burrowing lifestyle. Their podia cover only the top and bottom of their bodies. Mainly being deposit feeders, sand dollars have a less developed Aristotle's lantern than that of the echinoids. In contrast, members of Class Holothuroidea (the

Strongylocentrotus droebachiensis **occurs throughout the northern temperate and arctic regions. Hannah Robinson.**

sea cucumbers) are elongate and have a crown of tentacles (actually modified tube feet) surrounding the mouth. The tentacles, which are used mainly for feeding, may be fingerlike or branched. They differ significantly from all fellow echinoderms in that their vascular system is filled with body fluid rather than seawater (they have no sieve plate). Primitive (especially burrowing) forms have the standard five longitudinal rows of podia, though this number is reduced to three in more advanced forms that move over hard surfaces on their sides. Some are known to secrete noxious chemicals when agitated.

Phylum Ectoprocta (the bryozoans) are found in nearly all shallow marine habitats. Most of the 4,000 species of ectoprocts are sedentary and colonial. They are adapted to exploit hard surfaces. The bryozoan body is made up of a polypide and cystid. The polypide is a package containing a feeding structure, digestive tract, muscles and nerves. Its feeding structure (referred to as a lophophore) is essentially a crown of ciliated tentacles; food particles are carried by tiny cilia to the mouth. The cystid is a tough casing that serves as the body wall. Each individual (referred to as a zooid) is confined to a thin exoskeleton (or zoecium). The zoecium is secreted by the epidermis. Depending upon the species, it may be composed of chitinous, calcareous or even gelatinous materials and may be tubular, oval, vase-like or box-like in shape. Colonies may be round, flat, folios or plumose in shape. While colonies can reach widths of over a meter, each individual is usually no more than 0.5 millimeters in length. Bryozoans function somewhat like little jack-in-the-boxes, popping open to feed on microplankton (especially bacteria and unicellular algae), and then quickly withdrawing into the zoecium for rest or protection. Though colonies are mostly made up of feeding zooids, modified zooids that are shaped like a bird beak may be present; these attack any small organism that may attempt to settle over or near the colony.

Bryozoans are common in coldwater habitats and may find their way into aquaria as hitchhikers on shells, sea weeds or live rock (where they are commonly mistaken for hydrozoa or even algae). Unfortunately, they have a dismal record of survivability in captivity. It appears that strong water movement and a generous supply of phytoplankton is critical for even short-term success with these unusual creatures. The staghorn bryozoan (*Heteropora* sp.) reportedly does well in captivity; feathery or lacy forms (*Bugula*, *Phidolopora*, etc.) have a less encouraging record at this time (Anderson, 2001). Wrobel (1991) suggests obtaining only freshly collected and carefully handled specimens that are whole and undamaged for the best chance of success.

Intelligent and capable of inflicting serious injury, the giant Pacific octopus (GPO) is an animal to be handled only by those who know what they are doing. Kenneth Wingerter.

Top snails (*Calliostoma annulatum*) on an unidentified bryozoan. Chad King.

Though some of its representatives appear to be quite simple, Phylum Chordata is the most advanced group of organisms on Earth. It is perhaps also the most morphologically and behaviorally diverse and is accordingly broken into several subdivisions. There are two major groups. Group Protochordata includes the subphyla Urochordata (the tunicates) and Cephalochordata (the lancelets); Group Craniata includes only one subphylum, Vertebrata (the fishes, amphibians, reptiles, birds and mammals). All are believed to have descended from a common, free-swimming chordate ancestor. The perforated protochordate pharynx that originated as a filter-feeding mesh serves as an exemplar for the eventual development of true internal gills.

All chordates possess—either in early development or throughout their life—a structure referred to as a notochord. The notochord is a semi-rigid rod enclosed in a tough sheath that runs along the length of the animal internally. It lends skeletal support by stiffening the body. It can also provide a means of locomotion; when pulled by muscular action, the notochord bends, generating an undulating movement. The notochord remains in protochordates and primitive vertebrates throughout their life, whereas in the majority of higher vertebrates the notochord is at some point replaced by a series of cartilaginous or bony vertebrae. A tubular nerve cord runs dorsally along the notochord, ending in an enlargement at the anterior end to form a brain. In vertebrates, the nerve cord is protected by the vertebrae while the brain is protected by a cartilaginous or bony structure (or cranium). Yet one more unique feature of Chordata is a postanal tail. Along with the bowing of the notochord, movement of the tail provides locomotion to larval tunicates and amphioxus during free-swimming stages of development.

There are approximately 1,500 tunicate species. The name of the group comes from the sturdy, nonliving, cellulose-based test (or tunic) that covers the animal. Though strictly marine, they are found in every corner of the ocean. While some are free-swimming throughout their entire lives (salps, larvaceans, etc.), most eventually settle and permanently assume a sessile lifestyle. The nerve cord is reduced to a single ganglion, and the notochord and tail completely disappear, during adult metamorphosis. As adults, the benthic tunicates (or ascidians) eventually take on a globular or cylindrical form. Ascidians may occur as solitary individuals, colonies or compounds. Water moves in and out of the animal through incurrent and excurrent siphon (earning them the common term sea squirt). As water enters the incurrent siphon, it passes through gill slits in a ciliated pharynx before spilling into a chamber (or atrial cavity) and exiting via the excurrent siphon. Food particles are collected in mucus on the endostyle, a ciliated groove at the back of the pharynx.

Much like clownfishes, juvenile *Oxylebius pictus* hide amongst the tentacles of certain *Urticina* spp. anemones. NOAA.

***Anthopleura* spp. should be provided with a light intensity of at least 73 $\mu mol/meter^2/second$. Claire Fackler.**

***Phyllopteryx taeniolatus* would be an incredibly poor choice of fish to stock with stinging cnidarian species. Tim Sheerman-Chase.**

Lipophrys nigriceps is an excellent choice for small warm-temperate systems. Stefano Guerrieri.

Caesioperca lepidoptera is found in small groups at depths down to about 100 meters (328 feet). Ian Skipworth.

The pelvic fins of *Eumicrotremus orbis* are modified into adhesive discs with which it firmly sucks to hard substrata. David Csepp.

Subphylum Cephalochordata appears to be a transitional form between protochordates and primitive fishes. Lancelets are translucent, slender, laterally compressed creatures that vaguely resemble a fish. They indeed share many similarities (structure of musculature, liver, etc.) with fish and other vertebrates. The group is small (about 25 species). They are little in size (around 5-7 centimeters (2-3 inches) in length) and are found in sandy soft-bottom habitats where they partially burrow into the substrate with their tail. Driven by action of cilia in the mouth (or buccal cavity), water is driven through gill slits in the pharynx. Food particles from the water column are trapped in mucus and moved by other cilia into the intestine. The filtered water then moves into an atrium and exits through a structure referred to as an atriopore.

The protochordates are not yet common in the aquarium trade. Still, tunicates are plentiful in cooler waters and could become more available as coldwater livestock supply chains continue to develop. Aside from use as laboratory animals, cephalochordates (e.g. *Amphioxus*) are seldom kept in aquaria, though they do have potential as refugium subjects. Fish, of course, have represented Subphylum Vertebrata in aquaria since the earliest days of aquarium keeping.

Vertebrates share basic chordate features with the other two subphyla but have certain characteristics of their own. They are unique in having a spinal column as well as a complete digestive system, skin comprised of both an epidermis and an inner dermis, paired kidneys, an endocrine system, a ventral heart, well-developed musculature, paired limbs and a highly differentiated brain. The largest and oldest vertebrate group, the fishes, claims as many as 22,000 living species. Per the definition given by eminent ichthyologist Karl Lagler (1962), fish are "cold-blooded animals, typically with backbones, gills, and fins, and are primarily dependent on water as a medium in which to live." Beyond that, they differ widely in terms of size, shape, behavior and favored habitat. There are three major divisions of the living fishes: (1) Class Agnatha (lampreys and hagfishes) which have pouched gills and lack jaws, (2) Class Chondrichthyes (sharks, rays, skates and their relatives) which have plated gills, a cartilaginous skeleton and a true jaw and (3) Class Osteichthyes (bony fishes) which have hardened gill plates (or opercula) and firm axial skeletons consisting of a skull, vertebral column, ribs and intermuscular bones. The ray-finned fishes (Class Osteichthyes, Subclass Actinopterygii) are by far the most numerous. Most members of this gigantic group are perch-like (or percoid) fishes, the Perciformes. The percoid marine fishes (typified by the sea basses (Serranidae)) have ctenoid scales, pelvic fins and a combination of hard and soft fin rays.

The fishes can be placed into three major zoographic categories: (1) shore or shelf fishes, including species that occur from the shoreline to depths of around 100 fathoms (200 meters (656 feet)), (2) open sea or pelagic fishes, including species that live near the surface and far from the shoreline and (3) abyssal fishes, including species that inhabit depths of over 100 fathoms. Well over half of the known marine fishes are shore-dwelling forms. Unlike the freshwater fishes, marine fishes are not so tightly restricted in distribution by physical barriers; really, temperature is the most important factor limiting the dispersal of marine fish species.

Scartella cristata **can be used to control filamentous algae. Stefano Guerrieri.**

Biogeographers place tropical shorefish faunas into four categories (Indo-Pacific, West Indian, West African and Panamanian). These bear much more resemblance to each other than any does to its neighboring temperate fauna. Subtropical fauna is essentially a diluted tropical fauna; restricted in distribution by an annual minimum temperature of 16-18°C (60-65°F), it has more in common with its tropical than its temperate neighbors. Whereas the biogeographic divisions between the tropical and temperate fishes are rather sharp, strong currents and seasonal variation makes the boundary between temperate and polar regions much less distinct. Fishes such as cod (Gadidae), herring (Clupeidae) and flatfish (Pleuronectiformes) are common in the higher latitudes. Though they may be abundant in terms of population size, the temperate and polar fish faunas are conspicuously less diverse than those of the tropics. Conversely, temperate fish communities vary from one another to a notably greater degree than do those of their tropical neighbors.

Chaetodon daedalma **is among the hardiest of the butterflyfishes. Felicia McCaulley.**

The North Pacific Ocean contains numerous endemic genera and claims one of the richest fish faunas outside of the Indo-Pacific. Many sculpins (Cottidae), rockfishes (Scorpaenidae), poachers (Agonidae), surf perches (Embriotocidae), snailfishes (Cyclopteridae) and greenlings (Hexagrammidae) reside there. North Atlantic fish faunas are remarkably similar, though they tend to be more adapted to seasonal fluctuation of water temperature. Due to bipolar routes of dispersal, northern temperate genera appear in some of the southern temperate regions. North Atlantic isotherms are set widely apart by great oceanic currents. As there is comparatively less diversion of oceanic currents by land masses, isotherms are much closer to parallel across southern temperate zones. The southern boundary with Antarctica lies at the 6° isotherm. The temperate South Pacific encompasses southern South America, South Africa and parts of Australia and New Zealand. This is home to fishes such as the John Dory (*Zeus faber*), wrasses (Labridae), perches (Serranidae and Callanthiidae), demoiselles and clownfishes (Pomacentridae), triplefins (Tripterygiidae) and maomao (Kyphosidae). While temperate Australia and New Zealand claim some endemic fish species, there is (particularly in New Zealand) an obvious relationship to both Chilean and Antarctic forms.

5. Livestock Acquisition

Many coldwater marine aquarium species can be obtained through the ornamental fish trade. Traditionally, aquarium specimens are obtained by sale at small, local fish stores (LFSs). Increasingly, aquarium livestock is sold through chain-like pet stores and web-based merchants. Be wary of some bigger, department store-like shops, which have a record of substandard livestock quality and inadequately trained salespeople. The attraction to online retailers is understandable, as they oftentimes have great selections of livestock virtually at your fingertips. And, as many hobbyists may be quick to point out, they typically sell at rock-bottom prices. In the main, that much is all true, and when the merchant is competent and honest, you can indeed find very good value online. That being said, the soundest source for your regular livestock purchases is a reputable saltwater-specialized LFS. It is only at a brick-and-mortar location that buyers can closely examine—even interact with—potential purchases. By closely scrutinizing the overall condition of the animals and their living conditions, you will rather quickly determine whether or not a dealer is worth your dollar.

Your readiness to buy a particular specimen should have less to do with price, health "guarantees" or your simple desire to have it, and more with its health and appropriateness for your particular system. It is highly advisable to not buy an animal until you have observed it feeding; be sure to purchase the very same food along with any animal you buy. Better retailers agree to hold livestock (typically with a partial or full down payment) for some short amount of time (maybe as long as a week). Try to back out of "holds" as seldom as possible (and even then only for good reason). Should a held item die or become ill, do not argue with a dealer that insists on refunding the down payment as a store credit, as they have just absorbed what would have been your loss. If the store offers any guarantee on live purchases, report only legitimate, qualifying losses for credit or refund. It is just as important for you to gain your dealer's trust and respect as it is for them to gain yours. Practicing good etiquette will get you much further along than any amount of skill, money, or luck ever will.

Hatfield Marine Science Center aquarists receive a giant Pacific octopus from local fishermen. Kenneth Wingerter.

It is possible in some regions (at least with the right permits) to harvest one's own aquarium livestock from the natural environment. This not only makes for a rather fun experience but also affords an intimate and gainful glimpse into the animal's microhabitat (be prepared to test collection sites for temperature, salinity, dissolved oxygen, pH, nitrate, etc.). That notwithstanding, collecting your own specimens requires a considerable amount of planning and resources. Planning for a collecting trip should begin days or weeks in advance. This gives the collector plenty of opportunity to (1) calculate travel times, (2) review fishing regulations, (3) print out detailed maps, (4) research the native biota and (5) check local tide tables and weather forecasts for each collection site. The extra time can also allow groups (e.g. marine aquarium clubs) to better schedule and corroborate their efforts. For safety, it is a good idea to arrange for at least one other adult to come along to act as a spotter; rather than assist with the collecting, they are there primarily to keep track of the tides and watch for dangerous sneaker waves.

Planning ahead also leaves time to inspect and prepare the collection gear. Many items will be required for harvest and transport. Harvesting tools will vary greatly with what is being collected. Depending upon the target species, mobile specimens may be captured by hand, dip net, seine net, trawl, dredge, trap or even rod and reel. Hard sessile invertebrates (e.g. *Caryophyllia smithii*) are best removed from their substrate with a sharp, slender chisel while softer types such as sea anemones are best removed with a somewhat softer and duller edge such as a small plastic paint scraper or old credit card. A powerful, water-resistant flashlight can be extremely handy while pursuing and capturing marinelife.

Good transport equipment will allow you to harvest more stuff and move it across greater distances. Large beverage coolers are well suited as main transport vessels. Each specimen should be transported in its own container. Such containers can be made from plastic food jars with numerous drilled holes. Sealed cold packs will be needed to maintain a low temperature. Do not use bare ice for this, as it will reduce the transport water salinity as it melts. Tap water can be frozen and sealed in soda bottles in a pinch, though a sturdy, hard plastic, refrigerant gel-filled cold pack will usually do the best job. Aeration should be supplied via a portable air pump. Live rock can be loosely wrapped in an old shower curtain rather than submerged in a cooler (throw a cold pack in there somewhere). Old, light-colored towels and/or blankets can be thrown over the transport containers in order to shield them from any direct sunlight that makes it through the car windows.

It is best to try to arrive at the collection site a bit early. This allows more time to set up, get in your waders, grab a bite to eat, etc. at a leisurely pace before getting to work. And, around one hour prior to low-tide, many creatures can be most easily captured as they retreat into the last few feet of ebb. The best time to collect in tidepools is during minus tides when tidal height is below the mean low water level.

One should practice good etiquette when working in the field. This requires some degree of conscientiousness and common sense. For example, one should walk carefully over the intertidal zone, not only for his or her own safety, but also to avoid trampling seaweeds and

Beverage coolers work well for transporting small specimens. Kenneth Wingerter.

This *Liparis florae* has been captured with a beach seine. David Ayers.

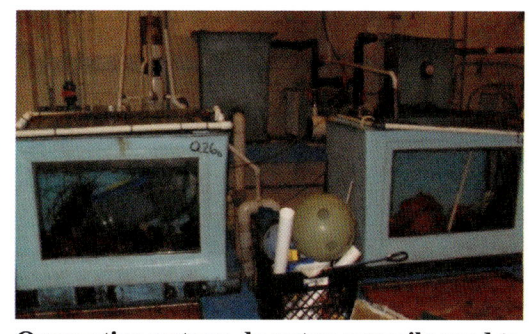

Quarantine systems do not necessarily need to look pretty; they do need to be in an area that is relatively quiet but checked often. Kenneth Wingerter.

delicate sedentary animals on the rocky surfaces. Overturned rocks should be put back exactly as they were found. One should not remove from the wild any organism without (1) adequately researching the captive care of the species and (2) having previously made all necessary preparations to house it. And, obviously, it is imperative that any collectors of wildlife (whether commercial, academic or private) fully understand and comply with all state and federal fishing regulations. Introduced species have become a serious problem in some areas; one should know how to identify them and, if possible, report their presence (especially if it is previously unknown in the area) to the appropriate state agency. Due to the risk of spreading novel pathogens, do not ever release a captive animal (even if it came from the very same area) back into the wild.

Multiple small containers can be carried about in a bucket while hand collecting small items in the intertidal zone. The bucket should be white as to absorb the least amount of solar energy. Flush the contents of the bucket with fresh, cool seawater often. Jackman (1975) alternatively suggests making a sort of "collecting box" that can be slung over the shoulder to free both hands. To minimize stress on the captured creatures, take only a modest load and promptly transport it to the home tank or holding facility.

6. Acclimation, Quarantine and Conditioning

Compared to their terrestrial counterparts, marine organisms live in a fairly stable physical and chemical environment and are thus ill-equipped to adapt physiologically to rapid environmental change. To avoid shocking aquarium animals while transferring them between different waters, one must allow them to undergo a process of acclimation. Acclimation techniques vary widely, but most involve slowly adding small volumes of water from the new system to the animal's transport water. This makes for a more gradual and protracted transition into the new environment. Acclimation should be carried out in a quiet, dimly lit area to avoid startling timid animals. Each specimen should be acclimated in its own space (bucket, compartment etc.). Cover the container (*not* airtight) when acclimating jumpy fishes or crawly crabs; the shade alone will calm them much. Acclimation is one of the most stressful ordeals a captive marine animal will have to face. Therefore, the gentlest of acclimation methods are best. Drip acclimation methods are ideal. A drip rig might consist of nothing more than a length of airline tubing, an airline valve (to control drip rate), some number of buckets and a small clamp to hold the rig in place. A manifold may be incorporated to feed multiple drip lines. The rig is made to siphon (drop by drop) into the acclimation containers. The best drip rate will depend upon things like starting volume of transport water, species sensitivity, etc., but might be something around a couple of drops per second when starting with a volume of a couple liters. When the transport water has been thoroughly diluted with the new water, the animal can be gently scooped or netted from the container and placed into its new home. Try to transfer as little transport water into the tank as possible.

The proper introduction of a new specimen to an established aquarium system is a necessarily elaborate process. Oftentimes, recent acquisitions are acutely stressed due to handling and transport. If they have been in the supply chain for very long, they might be starved or malnourished. They may bear injuries inflicted during harvest or while being held with aggressive tankmates. And, perhaps most importantly, they may be harboring disease organisms. For all of these reasons and more, any serious aquarist will quarantine and condition new specimens before introducing (much less exposing) them to the main system. This is so whether or not the animal shows any outward signs of stress, injury or illness. The difference between quarantine and conditioning is simple; quarantine involves temporarily isolating an animal (and any associated disease organisms) from the general animal population whereas conditioning involves actions taken to restore a distressed animal to an optimal state of health. Conditioning primarily serves to protect a new specimen while quarantine primarily serves to protect the rest of the collection. In most circumstances, both processes are carried out simultaneously. The main idea is to make the animal's transition from the dealer/natural environment to your aquarium system as safe, relaxed and comfortable as possible. The benefits of a sensible quarantine (or QT) procedure are numerous. Most obviously, it allows the new animal to be closely monitored for any health concerns that may arise. It cannot be attacked by other animals and can easily hide/rest while it recuperates. Kept in isolation, animals in quarantine are more easily made to resume (or catch up on) feeding. Reluctant fish or crustaceans will be able to take food items at their own pace. Sessile filter feeders can be generously spot fed to rebuild depleted energy stores. Medications may be used without the risk of harming other animals or being prematurely removed via skimming, carbon, etc.

It is always a good idea to take whatever data you can from each collection site. Jon Olav Bjørndal.

Too often, quarantine set-ups are undersized, inadequately filtered and poorly maintained; the result is undue stress on an already stressed-out animal. In actual fact, QT water quality should meet or exceed that of the main system. At least as far as the quarantined animal is concerned, it can be worse to cut corners during quarantine than to skip it altogether. The only way to do it right (at a minimum) is to provide the animal with consistently clean seawater as well as ample space to stretch out or hide. Quarantine should be carried out in a quiet area where the inhabitant will not be constantly disturbed by movement and noises from outside the tank. Aesthetics are utterly unimportant here. To facilitate cleaning the enclosure and observing the animal, the most effective QT set-up is bare-bottom with no significant hardscape. Animals that require a hide can be accommodated with one or more sections of PVC pipe of an appropriated length and diameter. Untreated terracotta pots can serve as caves for

Sections of banded PVC pipe make a simple, clean, cheap aquascape of sorts for holding tanks containing small, territorial fishes such as *Meiacanthus kamoharai*. Kenneth Wingerter.

larger specimens. Additional cover can provided by a few plastic or silk aquarium plants. To ease stress for exceptionally shy creatures, painter's tape can be applied to the parts of the front and/or side tank panels for extra privacy (without seriously impeding the keeper's view). Unless housing photosynthetic organisms (e.g. kelps or zooxanthellate anemones), lighting should be minimal if used at all.

Quarantine systems may be operated either as needed or on a continual basis. In the former case, it is preferable to employ simple (though powerful) filtration with minimal plumbing (e.g. large canister filters). Though this approach conserves space and operating expense, it is not ideal. The latter case is preferable for two reasons. First, a continuously operated system will be available for immediate use—not a bad thing when tending to an urgent situation. Furthermore, it will (so long as it has been fully cycled) be far more capable of managing the inhabitant's nitrogenous wastes. Particularly if the animal is being fed heavily, critical water parameters (ammonia, pH, etc.) should be very closely monitored throughout the entire quarantine period.

To avoid cross contamination, the keeper must practice good biosecurity when working between the quarantine and main system. Feeding tongs, algae scrapers, even one's own hands may transfer pathogens from one system to the other. A physical object that acts as a means of transport for an infectious organism is referred to as a fomite. Potential fomites can be eliminated by completely sterilizing aquarium tools between uses or (better yet) keeping a dedicated set of tools for each system. Keepers should wash up well when working between multiple systems or (better yet) try to work on only one system on any given day. If a keeper must work on multiple tanks on the same day, it is safest to work first on the main tank(s) and then on the QT tank. The use of an ultraviolet sterilizer (sized for true sterilization rather than mere clarification) can greatly enhance biosecurity. A tight lid should be placed on the QT tank to keep the animal in as well as exclude any fomites (including spray from the main tank, if nearby).

Collected from very deep waters, *Gonioplectrus hispanus* may suffer from serious decompression trauma and should be allowed to fully recuperate in QT before being introduced to the main tank. James Hoehlein.

Depending entirely upon individual circumstances, the duration of the quarantine and conditioning period might be as short as a week or as long as months. After being fully quarantined and conditioned, the animal will be ready for transfer to the main tank. Here, the acclimation process can be made a bit softer by performing a large (up to 50%) water change on the QT tank using water from the main system about 12-24 hours prior to the move. After being placed in its new home, the animal should be closely watched over the next few days for any signs of stress or harassment from its tankmates; if any problems arise, it should be immediately returned to quarantine until the issue is resolved.

Afterword

What a long, wonderful way we've come in keeping temperate marine aquaria. Not so long ago, we were ambitious marine aquarists looking for a challenging new biotope to keep in our homes; and what could be more challenging than doing something few others had ever done? At the time, the resources and knowledge we had available to us were diminutive at best. A few articles, a website or two, a couple people who had kept these systems in the past. Luckily, the few people we found that helped us along the way are some of the most dedicated and knowledgeable around in the field of temperate home aquarium keeping.

Sourcing livestock, finding suitable chillers, tanks, filtration, lighting, just about every aspect of it was either a word of mouth telling or a trial and error experience until now. We remember scouring lists of wholesale fish dealers hoping for the rare chance that a cool water oddity might have made its way into the tropical aquarium trade for us to save. We emailed countless public aquariums looking for leads on potential sources for temperate livestock, just to be disappointed when we were told that they were only sold "for scientific purposes."

Coldwater aquaria are addictive; fish tanks can soon turn into fish rooms. Kenneth Wingerter.

Nonetheless, we were not deterred. We started collecting livestock for ourselves, and eventually obtained commercial permits to begin collecting and selling to other temperate hobbyists. Since then, the number of coldwater aquarium keepers has been growing exponentially, and with it so has the vast cumulative knowledge gained and shared by those individuals. Numerous sources for livestock have begun popping up, along with specialized aquarium systems designed to keep cool water species that come ready to go right out of the box. Now that this book has filled in the last missing piece needed for all coldwater keepers (an at-your-fingertips, all-encompassing temperate water resource), the barriers that we had to endure just to keep a few native species are all but gone. Looking back, it was an adventurous way to learn how to do something with all those obstacles in the way. But if hindsight is 20/20, *The Coldwater Marine Aquarium* puts things perfectly in perspective.

Growing up near the Oregon coast definitely has its perks, with unlimited access to some of the best tidepools that the U.S. Pacific Northwest has to offer. We quickly became obsessed with marine biology at a very young age. Years ago, we only dreamed of keeping temperate

Once quite rare, coldwater livestock is showing up in the trade with greater regularity. Here, Stu Wobbe shows off a newly imported weedy seadragon. Josh Groves.

marine aquaria in our own homes, let alone somehow finding our way into the marine aquarium hobby and then becoming collectors of temperate marine livestock for retail sales, public aquariums and scientific research. Co-owning a collection company together has been one of the best experiences we've had in our lives thus far. Getting the chance to travel across the U.S. speaking for conferences, zoos and classrooms as well as showing off coldwater livestock to the general public is beyond belief!

Being among the few people involved in the temperate marine hobby has meant that coming up with information pertaining to the husbandry, ecology and the biology of these animals in public and home aquaria wouldn't always be easy. It's not that the information isn't there if you go looking for it, but that in doing so one could easily get lost in a sea of information strewn about textbooks and multiple websites (if you're lucky enough to find them). So a good portion of the last six years of our lives has been dedicated to answering questions regarding where to look up this information as well as building our company's own library of scientific papers, biology books and online blogs. The future of temperate marine aquarium keeping will be dictated mainly by the amount of useful information that can be easily obtained so that one might be able to successfully keep these biotopes alive and thriving—the goal that we all strive to reach. If those who share a passion for marine biology keep pushing the limits to keep this information available and fresh, many more generations of people will be able to enjoy niche hobbies like temperate aquarium keeping.

In closing, we feel that the coldwater hobby will continue to grow in the coming years, with many more collection companies springing up and lots of livestock offerings from places we only dreamed of before (Australia, Japan, and Europe, to name a few) along with countless new coldwater specialized products. This will make it even easier for people to successfully replicate what could before only be enjoyed at a public aquarium, keeping these systems in their own homes and finding so much joy in this cold, colorful biotope.

Lush "planted" tanks could become commonplace with the increased cultivation of ornamental macroalgae. Michiel Vos.

Cutting-edge LFSs have begun to display rare temperate species (such as this male *Aracana ornata* at House of Fins) in their show tanks. Joe Mulvey.

Stu Wobbe and Josh Groves (Coldwater Marine Aquatics), July 18, 2016.

Bibliography

[1] Anderson, Roland C., Ph.D. *Aquarium Husbandry of Pacific Northwest Marine Invertebrates*. Seattle, WA: Seattle Aquarium, 2001.
[2] Ayling, Tony. *Collins Guide to the Fishes of New Zealand*. Auckland, NZ: William Collins Publishers, Ltd., 1982.
[3] Bertness, Mark D. *Marine Community Ecology*. Sunderland, MA: Sinauer Associates, Inc., 2001.
[4] Bjørndal, Jon Olav. *Jon Olavs Akvarium*. http://www.jonolavsakvarium.com.
[5] Bjørndal, Jon Olav. "Where Change is Constant: The "Seasonal" Color Displays in a Macroalgae Setup Might Make Reef Aquarists Envious." *FAMA* 32 (12). December, 2009.
[6] Bjørndal, Jon Olav. "Chillers: A Need-to-Know Primer." *Coral 11*(3), May/June 2014.
[7] Brightwell, Chris. *The Nano-Reef Handbook: The Ultimate Guide to Reef Systems Under 15 Gallons*. Neptune City, NJ: T.F.H. Publications, Inc., 2006.
[8] Burgess, Warren E., Dr., Dr. Herbert R. Axelrod and Raymond E. Hunziker III. *Dr. Burgess's Atlas of Marine Aquarium Fishes*. 3rd ed. Neptune City, NJ: T.F.H. Publications, Inc., 1990.
[9] Campbell, Neil A. and Jane B. Reece. *Biology*. 6th ed. San Francisco, CA: Benjamin Cummings, 2002.
[10] Chave, E.H. and Alexander Malahoff. *In Deeper Waters: Photographic Studies of Hawaiian Deep-Sea Habitats and Life-Forms*. Honolulu, HI: University of Hawaii Press, 1998.
[11] Coleman, Neville. *1001 Nudibranchs: Catalogue of Indo-Pacific Sea Slugs*. Springwood, Australia: Neville Coleman's Underwater Geographic Pty Ltd, 2001.
[12] Clipperton, John. "The Goldilocks Zone." *Ultramarine*, issue 52, June-July 2015.
[13] Dawson, E. Yale. *Marine Botany: An Introduction*. New York, NY: Holt, Rinehart and Winston, Inc., 1966.
[14] Delbeek, J. Charles and Julian Sprung. *The Reef Aquarium: Science, Art, and Technology*. Volume three. Coconut Grove, FL: Ricordea Publishing, 2005.
[15] Denny, Mark. *How the Ocean Works: An Introduction to Oceanography*. Princeton, NY: Princeton University Press, 2008.
[16] Desonie, Dana, Ph.D. *Biosphere: Ecosystems and Biodiversity Loss*. New York, NY: Chelsea House Publishers, 2008.
[17] Dring, M.J. *The Biology of Marine Plants*. Cambridge, U.K.: Cambridge University Press, 1992.
[18] Dufault, Aaron. "Coldwater Systems: Showcasing Life from the Frigid Waters of Puget Sound." *Coral 11*(3), May/June 2014.
[19] Freeman, Scott. *Biological Science*. Upper Saddle River, NJ: Prentice-Hall, 2002.
[20] Godshall, Danielle. "8 Tips for Creating a Coldwater Marine Tank." *Fish Channel*. Retrieved April 29, 2016. http://www.fishchannel.com/setups/saltwater/how-to-create-a-coldwater-marine-system.aspx.
[21] Hargreaves, Vincent. *The Complete Book of the Marine Aquarium*. San Diego, CA: Thunder Bay Press, 2006.
[22] Hemdal, Jay F. *Advanced Marine Aquarium Techniques*. Neptune City, NJ: T.F.H. Publications, Inc., 2006.
[23] Herald, Earl. *Fishes of North America*. Garden City, NY: Doubleday & Company, Inc., 1972.
[24] Hickman, Cleveland P. Jr., Larry S. Roberts and Allan Larson. *Integrated Principles of Zoology*. 9th ed. Dubuque, IA: Wm. C. Brown Publishers, 1993.
[25] Hoffman, Jennifer. *Ocean Sciences*. New York, NY: HarperCollins Publishers, 2007.

[26] Holmes-Farley, Randy. "Silica in Reef Aquariums." *Advanced Aquarist* 2(1), January 2003. http://www.advancedaquarist.com/2003/1/aafeature1.
[27] Holmes-Farley, Randy. "Chemistry And The Aquarium: Iodine in Marine Aquaria: Part I." *Advanced Aquarist* 2(3), March 2003. http://www.advancedaquarist.com/2003/3/chemistry.
[28] Holmes-Farley, Randy. "Ammonia and the Reef Aquarium." *Reefkeeping* 2(17), 2007. http://reefkeeping.com/issues/2007-02/rhf/#17.
[29] Hunziker, Ray. *Marine Aquariums*. Irvine, CA: I-5 Publishing, 2005.
[30] Jackman, L.A. *Sea Water Aquaria*. First American ed. Cranbury, NJ: A.S. Barnes and Company, 1975.
[31] Kuiter, Rudie H. *Butterflyfishes, Bannerfishes and Their Relatives: A Comprehensive Guide to* Chaetodontidae *and* Microcanthidae. Chorleywood, UK: TMC Publishing, 2002.
[32] Lagler, Karl F., John E. Bardach and Robert R. Miller. *Ichthyology*. New York, NY: John Wiley & Sons, Inc., 1962.
[33] Levinton, Jeffrey S. *Marine Biology: Function, Biodiversity, Ecology*. 2nd ed. New York, NY: Oxford University Press, 2001.
[34] Marchand, Peter J. *Life in the Cold: An Introduction to Winter Ecology*. 3rd ed. Hanover, NH: University Press of New England, 1996.
[35] Meinkoth, Norman A. (Ed.). *National Audubon Society Field Guide to North American Seashore Creatures*. New York, NY: Chanticleer Press, Inc., 1981.
[36] Michael, Scott W. *Angelfishes and Butterflyfishes*. Neptune City, NJ: T.F.H. Publications, Inc., 2004.
[37] Michael, Scott W. *Wrasses and Parrotfishes: The Complete Illustrated Guide to Their Identification, Behaviors, and Captive Care*. Neptune City, NJ: T.F.H. Publications, Inc., 2009.
[38] Mills, Dick. *Tetra Encyclopedia of the Marine Aquarium*. Morris Plains, NJ: Tetra Press, 1987.
[39] Moe, Martin A. Jr. *The Marine Aquarium Reference: Systems and Invertebrates*. Plantation, FL: Green Turtle Publications, 1992.
[40] Mowka, Edmund J. Jr. *The Seawater Manual: Fundamentals of Water Chemistry for Marine Aquarists*. Mentor, OH: Aquarium Systems, Inc., 1981.
[41] National Oceanic and Atmospheric Administration. "Coastal Water Temperature Guide (CWTG)." https://www.nodc.noaa.gov/dsdt/cwtg.
[42] Nilsen, Alf Jacob and Svein A. Fossa. *Reef Secrets*. Neptune City, NJ: T.F.H. Publications, Inc., 2002.
[43] Northington, David K. and J.R. Goodin. *The Botanical World*. St. Louis, MO: Times Mirror/Mosby College Publishing, 1984.
[44] Omori, Makoto and Tsutomu Ikeda. *Methods in Marine Zooplankton Ecology*. New York, NY: John Wiley & Sons, Inc., 1984.
[45] Paletta, Michael. *The New Marine Aquarium*. Neptune City, NJ: T.F.H. Publications, Inc., 2001.
[46] Pentair Aquatic Eco-Systems. Master Catalog. 2016.
[47] Raven, Peter H. and George B. Johnson. *Biology*. 6th ed. New York, NY: McGraw-Hill, 2002.
[48] Riddle, Dana. "An Introduction, Care and Feeding of Zooxanthellae." *Advanced Aquarist* 8(11), November 2014. http://www.advancedaquarist.com/2014/11/aafeature.
[49] Riddle, Dana. "Moonlight - A Concise Review of Its Spectrum, Intensity, Photoperiod, and Relationship to Coral and Fish Spawning." *Advanced Aquarist* 11(7), July 2012. http://www.advancedaquarist.com/2012/7/lighting.

[50] Shimek, Ronald, PH.D. "Chilled Out." *Coral* 11(3), May/June 2014.
[51] Schoener, T.W. "Some Comments on Connell's and my Reviews of Field Experiments on Interspecific Competition." *American Naturalist* no. 125. 1985.
[52] Solomon, Eldra P., Linda R. Berg and Diana W. Martin. *Biology*. 6th ed. Thomson Learning, Inc., 2002.
[53] Stiling, Peter D. *Ecology: Theory and Applications*. 2nd ed. Upper Saddle River, NJ: Prentice-Hall, 1992.
[54] Thiel, Albert. *The Marine Fish and Invert Reef Aquarium*. Cornel, NY: Aardvark Press, 1989.
[55] Vos, Michiel. *An Bollenessor: Marine Life in Cornwall*. https://anbollenessor.wordpress.com. 2016.
[56]Waller, Geoffrey. *Sea Life: A Complete Guide to the Marine Environment*. Washington, D.C.: Smithsonian Institution Press, 1996.
[57] Walls, Jerry G. (Ed.). *Encyclopedia of Marine Invertebrates*. Neptune City, NJ: T.F.H. Publications, Inc., 1982.
[58] Waycott, Michelle, Kathryn McMahon and Paul Lavery. *A Guide to Southern Temperate Seagrasses*. Clayton, Australia: Csiro Publishing, 2014.
[59] Weast, Steve. *Oregon Reef: Coldwater System Details*. http://oregonreef.com/sub_coldwater.htm. 2004.
[60] Wingerter, Kenneth. "An Evaluation of Potentially Abiotic Factors in the Lateral Distribution of Mixed *Zostera marina* and *Zostera japonica* Beds in Yaquina Bay, Oregon." C… *The Journal of Aquatic Science, Travel, and Adventure* 2(3), 2007.
[61] Wingerter, Kenneth. "Try a Cool, Refreshing Temperate Marine Aquarium." *Advanced Aquarist* 3(3), May 2009. http://www.advancedaquarist.com/2009/3/aquarium.
[62] Wingerter, Kenneth. "Considerations for Building and Maintaining a Temperate Marine Aquarium." *Advanced Aquarist* 3(4), May 2009. http://www.advancedaquarist.com/2009/4/howto.
[63] Wingerter, Kenneth. "Prospective Livestock for the Temperate Marine Aquarium." *Advanced Aquarist* 3(5), May 2009. http://www.advancedaquarist.com/2009/5/short.
[64] Wingerter, Kenneth. "Collection and Aquarium Husbandry of Northeast Pacific Non-Photosynthetic Cnidaria." *Advanced Aquarist* 10(1), January 2011. http://www.advancedaquarist.com/2011/1/corals.
[65] Wingerter, Kenneth. "Disturbance-Facilitated Coexistence of Sessile Organisms in Space-Limited Environments: A Review of Works in Ecological Disturbance Theory." *Advanced Aquarist* 10(5), May 2011. http://www.advancedaquarist.com/2011/5/aafeature.
[66] Wingerter, Kenneth. "Prospective Fishes for the New Zealand Rocky Reef Aquarium: A Multimedia Overview." *Advanced Aquarist* 11(6), June 2012. http://www.advancedaquarist.com/2012/6/fish.
[67] Wingerter, Kenneth, Betty Mujica and Tim Miller-Morgan. *Development of Live Shellfish Export Capacity in Oregon*. Corvallis, Oregon: Sea Grant Oregon (Oregon State University), 2013.
[68] Wingerter, Kenneth. "Coldwater Coming." *Coral* 11(3), May/June 2014.
[69] Wingerter, Kenneth. "Deep Focus." *Coral* 11(3), May/June 2014.
[70] Wingerter, Kenneth. "On the Captive Biology of Tube Anemones." *Advanced Aquarist* 8(7), July 2014. http://www.advancedaquarist.com/2014/7/inverts.
[71] Wingerter, Kenneth. "All the Cool Stuff Comes from the Tropics… or Does it?" *Ultramarine* issue 51, April 2015.
[72] Woodward, Susan L. *Biomes of Earth: Terrestrial, Aquatic, and Human-Dominated*. West Port, CT: Greenwood Press, 2003.
[73] Wrobel, David. *The Temperate Reef Aquarium*. Sand City, CA: California Reef Specialists, 1991.

About the Author

Kenneth Wingerter has been keeping aquaria of all kinds for over 30 years. His interest in coldwater marine wildlife was sparked while working around Alaska and Siberia aboard a Bering Sea fishing vessel.

In later years, while studying in the Pacific Northwest United States, he started and operated foreshores.net, which was at the time the only temperate marine aquarium livestock specialty retail operation. Upon earning his Bachelor of Science Degree in Biology at the University of Oregon, he went on to focus his research on coldwater aquaria while acquiring certification in the Aquarium Science Program.

While working throughout the last two decades in the aquarium industry, Kenneth has had the opportunity to maintain public and private aquarium exhibits, oversee greenhouse and laboratory facilities and engage in intensive ornamental and sportfish aquaculture. He remains deeply and happily involved in the field of aquarium science as a contributor to a number of American and European aquarium hobbyist publications.

Printed in Great Britain
by Amazon